SECRETS

of the THIRD

HEAVEN

SECRETS

of the THIRD
HEAVEN

PERRY STONE

SECRETS OF THE THIRD HEAVEN

Published by Voice of Evangelism Ministries
P. O. Box 3595
Cleveland TN 37320
423.478.3456
www.perrystone.org

Unmarked Scripture quotations are from the King James Version of the Bible.

Scripture quotations marked NKJV are from the New Kings James Version of the Bible. Copyright © 1979, 1980, 1982 by Thomas Nelson, Inc., publishers. Used by permission.

First Edition © March 2020

Printed in the United States of America

ISBN: 978-0-9855372-7-2

Cover Design & Layout: Micahel Dutton

CONTENTS

WHEN YOU HAVE 4 SECONDS LEFT TO LIVE

Have you ever wondered what or how you would feel if you knew you were seconds away from dying? I have met several individuals who experienced this feeling. One is a ministry friend of mine who, many years ago, was the pastor at the Deland Church of God in Florida, where I ministered each year. On a Sunday afternoon, a friend invited him to a small local airport. They planned to ride in a special two-seater plane. Both men took their seats, placed headphones on their heads, and buckled up. As the plane sped down the runway and lifted into the air, suddenly, the pilot knew something was wrong. The rudder stuck, making it impossible to fly properly. The plane began veering to one side. The pilot yelled, "We have a problem! We are going to crash!"

The plane did crash. My friend, Mike Coleman, was unconscious, bruised but alive, and survived the frightening event along with the pilot. Afterward, while we were sitting in his church office, I asked him a question that I have always wanted to ask someone who stepped toward the edge of eternity, unexpectedly knowing they were about to die but were graced to return and talk about it. My question was,

"How much time did you have from the announcement that a crash was coming, to the time you struck the ground, and what went through your mind?"

He paused, thought, then answered, "I probably had about a good four seconds from the time the plane banked to one side until it hit the ground." It was his next statement that stunned me. He replied, "As far as what went through my mind... everything. It was as though my mind was the hard drive of a computer filled with information, and someone flipped a switch, causing my mind to release everything about my life, from my beginning until that moment before impact."

I asked him about the details that flooded his mind. He responded and said, "It started with me as a small boy, and in my mind, my entire life, both the good and bad flashed before me. I thought of my wife and wondered if she would remarry. I saw the faces of my two daughters flash before me and felt a sting of sadness because I would miss their graduation. I also recalled a check on my desk that was not signed that I should have signed. This download of my life all occurred within about four seconds."

When people are faced with sudden death, the thought of entering the mysterious realm of another world creates a different response among different types of people. There is evidence through various research I have conducted that those who have a strong belief in God, a personal relationship with Him, a connection with the Holy Scriptures, have a prayer life, and love their families, often experience a curious mix of anticipation and excitement, as they believe their soul and spirit will soon be with the Lord and their departed loved ones, in a far-away heavenly paradise.

There is, however, a different feeling that emerges in the room and in the hearts of those who have ignored spiritual matters all of their lives, living carnal and selfish, and hosting a life that is evil. There is a horrible sense of a dark foreboding, including a cloud of hopelessness that engulfs their soul. However, the good news for a righteous person *is they have no expiration date!*

I have preached messages and studied the afterlife from a Biblical perspective for many years. I recall when my beloved father passed away in a room at Life Care Centers of America in Cleveland, Tennessee. I walked into the room five minutes after he passed. His breath was gone, he laid in silent repose, and because of no blood flow, his body color changed to a gray ash color. I knew his spirit was gone. He had taken his journey to the other world, to a heavenly place where righteous spirits await the resurrection. At that moment, several questions overwhelmed my thoughts. At that time, I had studied the Bible for about 130,000 hours and had a detailed understanding of the human soul and spirit, death, and the world beyond. But new questions struck my conscience. I sat in a chair and thought, "Is his spirit still lingering in the room? Can he see the family gathered at his bedside? Does he remember earthly events, and will he ever be able to see anything on earth occurring in the future? Will he soon see the two children my mom miscarried? What about the baby my wife Pam lost? Are their small spirits waiting to meet him…"? It was then that I determined to explore, in greater detail, the life beyond this life.

I have taught and written on the subject of heaven in the past. However, so many new questions and insights developed from word studies that I knew it was time to expound on this subject, adding this new material and answering some very challenging questions. This book is a result of my many months of research. Hopefully, it will help the readers understand the *Secrets of the Third Heaven*, where the dead are, and what they know.

Living for Eternity,
Perry Stone, Jr.

CHAPTER ONE

CAUGHT UP TO THE THIRD HEAVEN

Throughout thousands of years of Biblical history, holy men have been privileged to pierce the veil of earth and enter the dimension of angels to see the secrets of heaven. The Bible teaches that there are different levels of heaven. The term "third heaven" is found only once in the Bible's sixty-six books. The phrase was penned by the Apostle Paul, describing a strange experience, in which he either saw a stunning otherworld vision or through an "out of the body" experience, was lifted away from the terrestrial world into a heavenly dimension somewhere in the upper celestial regions. Paul called it the third heaven.

Here is his written account, found in 2 Corinthians 12:1-4 (NKJV):

"It is doubtless not profitable for me to boast. I will come to visions and revelations of the Lord: I know a man in Christ who fourteen years ago — whether in the body I do not know, or whether out of the body I do not know, God knows — such a one was caught up to the third heaven. And I know such a man — whether in the body or out of the body I do not know, God knows — how he was caught up into Paradise and heard inexpressible words, which it is not lawful for a man to utter."

This narrative requires a more detailed study. Paul was blessed to receive several *revelations* from the Lord that were hidden with God from the beginning of creation. He wrote, *"Even the mystery which has been hid from ages and from generations, but is now made manifest to his saints"* (Col. 1:26). One fascinating revelation Paul received concerned a future event that would suddenly occur. Those living on earth would hear a shout from the archangel, the blast of a loud shofar (trumpet–KJV), indicating Christ's return in which the living saints would instantly be changed from mortal to immortal (1 Cor. 15:52). Believers alive, at that time, will be "caught up" to meet the Lord in the air (1 Thess. 4:16-17). No Old Testament prophet, or early apostle, received this particular revelation, except Paul. It was Paul himself who acknowledged, "I come to visions and revelation from the Lord."

The forces of darkness are always threatened by spiritual revelation. Biblical revelation exposes the plots and strategies of God's enemies; thus, thwarting their plans. A divine revelation can change a person's earthly situation. The intensity of Paul's visions, dreams, and revelations was so astonishing. They became a threat to God's spiritual adversaries. To hinder the spread of these new truths that were exploding on earth through the Gospel, Satan commissioned a "thorn in the flesh, a messenger of Satan to buffet Paul" (2 Cor. 12:7).

The Greek word for *messenger* here is *aggelos*. It is found over 180 times in the Greek New Testament. In most cases, the word is translated as angel, and in 7 cases, it is translated in the KJV as messenger. It is the same Greek word used in Revelation chapters two and three, where Christ is addressing the pastors of the seven churches saying, "Unto the angel of the church at Sardis," and so forth (Revelation 2:1; 2:8; 2:12; 2:18). In these passages, the "angel" was a human messenger, the pastor of each church.

Paul's *messenger* was an *angel of Satan*. According to Scripture, Satan has an organized kingdom consisting of "principalities, powers, rulers of the darkness of this world, and wicked spirits in heavenly places" (Eph. 6:12). This particular evil messenger, or angel, was given the assignment to continually "buffet" Paul (2 Cor. 12:7).

The Greek word for buffet means to *keep slapping, or dealing one blow after another.* The imagery is a man in a boxing ring fighting an opponent, in which the opposition is continually clipping him on the ear with a blow strong enough to knock him off balance. Paul was basically saying, "When I think I am standing up doing well, I am suddenly knocked down again and again." He would pick himself up, believing he was making progress, when out of nowhere, here came another blow.

In 2 Corinthians chapter eleven, prior to revealing this thorn in the flesh, Paul listed a series of obstacles he consistently encountered that slowed down his ministry, and caused him great pain physically, emotionally, and spiritually. The list includes 22 different trials and difficulties. Paul was on a satanic hit list aimed to stop his ministry. The book of Acts details many of the narratives Paul alluded to in his list recorded in 2 Cor. 11:23-28:

- Acts 9: His life was threatened in Damascus, and he escaped over the wall in a basket.

- Acts 13: Paul's message was rejected by the Jews, and he was accused of blasphemy.

- Acts 14: Paul was dragged out of the city of Lystra and was stoned.

- Acts 15: A strong contention arose between Paul and Barnabas that caused a division.

- Acts 16: Paul and Silas were arrested, beaten, and placed in prison.

- Acts 17: Paul's preaching caused an uproar at Thessalonica.

- Acts 18: Paul's message was rejected at Corinth. He was arrested and stood trial.

- Acts 19: A riot broke out at Ephesus after idol worshipers were converted to Christ.

- Acts 21: A riot broke out in the city, and Paul was arrested.

- Acts 22: Paul had to go to "court" for preaching the gospel.

- Acts 23: A group of zealous religious Jews sought to kill Paul.

- Acts 27: While on his way to Rome, Paul was in a severe shipwreck, yet survived.

- Acts 28: Paul was bitten by a deadly viper, yet miraculously survived.

This strong demonic spirit was an authorized demonic agent sent to create adverse circumstances against Paul and his ministry. *Why* the Lord permitted this entity to work against Paul should also be noted. The apostle wrote, "lest I should be exalted above measure through the abundance of the revelations," this "thorn in the flesh" was allowed (2 Cor. 12:7).

To prevent from personally boasting upon this amazing visitation to heaven, Paul wrote, "I knew a man." Scholars believe he is speaking of his own experience.

Paul said he was "caught up" into the third heaven. The Greek word is *harpazo* and is the same Greek word Paul penned when, at the return of Christ, he said that we shall be "caught up" to meet the Lord in the air (1 Thess. 4:17). This Greek word has several possible meanings, including "to snatch out by force, to suddenly rescue one from danger, and to remove from one location to another." The word indicates a very *quick and sudden* removal of a person from one locale to a new one. Paul was "caught up," meaning this was not a progressive or gradual snatching up but was immediate and swift. For example, in Luke 16, the moment the rich man died, he immediately, "in hell lifted up his eyes being in torments" (Luke 16:23). One moment he was in his home, ignoring a beggar at his gate and enjoying the easy life and the abundance acquired during his lifetime. Then suddenly, he blanked out (perhaps a heart attack), and seconds later, he lifted his head and his eyes, realizing he (his soul and spirit) was in another world.

The Apostle John demonstrated the *suddenness* of a spiritual vision. He was exiled on the Island of Patmos, when he was suddenly overcome by the presence of the Lord and was "in the Spirit" (Rev. 1:10), meaning his mind and eyes were alerted and opened to God's presence. He began experiencing a lengthy vision of God's plans for the future. He was writing on parchment, and at the same time, he was seeing something otherworldly. After receiving a message in vision form from Christ to release in writing to seven churches (Rev. 2-3), John heard a trumpet from heaven accompanied by a voice saying, "Come up here" (Rev. 4:1). Immediately, he was in God's eternal heavenly throne room, seeing God, Christ (the Lamb), and a multitude of worshippers with 24 elders sitting on thrones (Rev. 4-5). This swift and immediate earth to heaven shift is similar to the transfer of a believer from earth to heaven at the moment of death.

The division of the heavens into three distinct sections was established from the beginning of creation in the foreknowledge of God. The first level is found on earth and was given to the dominion of men. The second level is seen in the scripture that calls Satan the "prince of the power of the air" (Eph. 2:2). Scholars note that the Greek word *air* alludes to the area from the ground on earth to the clouds. However, all living and breathing beings can only go as high as the available oxygen. From that point, moving into the dark matter of space, the region of the sun, moon, and stars, only spirit-beings, both good (angelic) and bad (demonic) can function and operate throughout this vast space at the speed of thought. The Milky Way Galaxy is 100,000 light-years across, giving you an idea of the expanse of God's second heaven.

The third heaven has not and could not be discovered through a massive telescopic lens. The location of this heavenly cosmic border is myriads of light-years away and likely located in another galaxy beyond the edge of our own. Just as the earth has an ozone layer, an amazing covering that a spacecraft must pierce when exiting or reentering the atmosphere, there is some type of a boundary or veil that must be pierced when entering from one galaxy to the other.

The first heaven is given for man. The second heaven is presently the principality zone where an unknown number of satanic powers and chief spirits have access. This is proven when we read in Revelation of a future war in heaven between Michael and his angels and Satan and his angels. This future conflict will send Satan's dark forces spiraling from the second heaven, thrusting them to the earth (Rev. 12:7-10).

When my Father, Fred Stone, was called into the ministry in his late teens, he was blessed with a remarkable spiritual experience in which he saw the very edge of the third heaven. Somewhere beyond was the abode where the souls of the righteous dwell. He said, "While sitting in a white cane back chair, I felt a surge in my heart and suddenly slumped over. I thought I had a heart attack and had died. Immediately, my soul came out of my body, like taking a hand out of a glove. My soul (or spirit) was suddenly whisked through space so fast that I was in a fetal position and could feel the pressure of my ascent. When I stopped, I opened my eyes, and I was standing in an open space on absolutely nothing. I was surrounded by the most beautiful, royal blue color, unlike anything I have seen on earth. The blue skies on earth pale in comparison to the rich, deep blue color, surrounding the edge of heaven."

During Paul's third heaven experience, he visited a place he called paradise. This word paradise is only found in the New Testament three times. The first is found when Christ told the dying thief on the cross, "Today you shall be with me in paradise" (Luke 23:43). The second location is when Paul was "caught up...into paradise" (2 Cor. 12:4). John gives us the third reference when he mentions that overcoming saints will eat of the tree of life, "which is in the midst of the paradise of God" (Rev. 2:7).

In human history, there have actually been two different locations for paradise. After Adam's sin, the souls of all men and women (both righteous and unrighteous) at death, descended under the crust of the earth to a place called Abraham's bosom, a massive underworld chamber where righteous souls remained until the resurrection of Christ (Luke 16:22). This underground paradise was populated for about four thousand years. Once Christ gained complete authority over death, hell, and the grave at His resurrection, all future righteous souls (at death) would be carried by angels to the third heaven paradise, the one Paul toured during his experience.

The Greek word that references paradise in the New Testament means *a park, an orchard, a garden.* The original concept of paradise would be the description of the Garden of Eden, the beautiful, perfect, earthly home God created for Adam. In Eden, the tree of life was located in the "midst" of the garden (Gen. 2:9). In the heavenly paradise, the tree of life is also in the "midst of the paradise of God" (Rev. 2:7). The word "midst" in Revelation 2:7 literally means "the middle." We would say the tree of life is placed in the center of both Eden and the third heaven paradise. The name "tree of life" has the word "life" in it. In Hebrew, the root of the word can mean "to cause to live." That is the best description of this tree because its fruit caused Adam and Eve to continually live. In the heavenly paradise, the tree of life yields twelve different types of fruit each month, and the leaves are eaten for the purpose of bringing healing (Rev. 22:2).

This heavenly paradise is what I call a "holding area." A weak illustration is that of a patient who must sit for an unknown amount of time in a waiting room with others until their name is called. They wait to see the physician who, after an examination, makes a judgment on their health. Millions of souls are now resting and waiting in paradise until their names are called in the resurrection, and they are released from this holding place to appear before the Judgment Seat of Christ.

What makes Paul's encounter with paradise very curious is when he wrote he had "heard unspeakable words which it was not lawful for a man to utter" (2 Cor. 12:4). Theologians have dissected this statement for centuries. It begs the question, what did Paul hear that was so dramatic, mysterious, and amazing, that he was instructed not to relate what he heard? The word *unspeakable* here alludes to *unworthiness, or undeserving.* Not being "lawful to utter" simply means "it is just not right to talk in public about what I heard." Paul was saying, "I was not worthy to see or hear what I saw and heard."

It is possible that there are several reasons for this statement. First, the incident may have been personally set up by God Himself to encourage Paul by revealing to him his future rewards if he would be faithful. Paul's suffering for Christ's sake (2 Cor. 11) may have required a time of encouragement about the good things to come for him in heaven. Thus, his conversation or words he heard were too personal to talk about since the theme here is Paul not being lifted up in pride through his amazing revelations. This was just for him to see, hear, and understand. A second opinion is that he was commanded by the Lord not to mention what he saw, and this could be for a simple reason. Those who have experienced any type of near-death encounter with angels or seeing heavenly realities, and begin telling their stories to others are often mocked and ridiculed by unbelieving sinners and Biblically illiterate Christians. Telling sacred God encounters or visions and being mocked by people is an example of "casting your pearl before swine," which Christ taught us to avoid (Matt. 7:6).

A third reason for avoiding a discussion concerning this dramatic paradise visit would be that many individuals living in his time or reading what he wrote may not have believed all that he reported concerning the mysteries of paradise. In the Bible, we read of prophets who penned details of the heavenly temple. They described the throne of God, revealed the types of angels, their strange wings and eyes, and detailed amazing insights to the reader of the gemstones, gates, and layers of the New Jerusalem. With much of heaven being seen in visions that were written about, it begs the question, what did Paul see that was so gripping and amazing, that he felt restrained to comment on it?

While there are numerous mysteries concerning the third heaven and paradise, I will explain the original meaning of certain Hebrew and Greek words. I will compare Scripture in both Testaments and sprinkle throughout the chapters, true stories from faithful and trusted believers to help answer as many questions as possible about the mysteries of the third heaven and heavenly realities, based upon what the Bible teaches.

CHAPTER TWO

INFORMATION TRANSFERS FROM EARTH TO HEAVEN

The death of a parent or a child is the most difficult emotion to experience. The thought of living on earth for many years and never seeing that loved one again plants an exceptional grief that practically no other human event does. Even more difficult than the earthly separation is the idea of that person having no memory of you or your family once they cross through the veil from death into eternity. What does the Bible teach about the knowledge the dead will have once they are in heaven? The future heavenly judgments hold the answers to this question.

Each person that has ever lived will, in the future, stand before God in His heavenly temple and be judged for their words spoken and deeds preformed while they lived on earth, including both the good and bad. Paul wrote:

> "For we must all appear before the Judgment Seat of Christ, that each one may receive the things done in the body, according to what he has done, whether good or bad."
>
> - 2 CORINTHIANS 5:10-11 (NKJV)

The phrase for judgment seat in the Greek is bema, a word commonly known in Paul's day. The *bema* was a raised platform built outside and made of stone. It was also an indoor wooden structure used by public officials who gave political speeches or heard legal cases. At times, Paul stood before a tribunal because he was accused of publicly promoting ideas contrary to the laws of the Jews (Acts 18:12-17). If the tribunal found him guilty, he would receive a penalty. If he was found innocent, he was released. In Acts 18, a judge refused to hear a case against Paul, leading to his release. The bema in Corinth, Greece, was erected around 44 B.C. and was constructed of beautiful blue and white marble.

The heavenly bema is where God's throne is positioned. It is surrounded by twenty-four elders who are sitting on smaller thrones. This "throne room" resides on a heavenly mountain identified as Mount Zion (Heb. 12:22 NKJV). In the future, 144,000 Jewish men will be caught up out of the Great Tribulation, appearing on this mountain with Christ. The mount alluded to in Revelation 14:1 is "Mount Zion." This will also be the location of two important heavenly judgments; the Bema or Judgment Seat of Christ (Rev. 11:18), and the Great White Throne judgment (Rev. 20:11).

Some believe that once our human soul and spirit exit the physical body at death, that any and all information connected with our earthly existence is somehow supernaturally erased when we enter the realm of heavenly knowledge. This is not what is taught in Scripture.

When two Old Testament prophets, Moses and Elijah, appeared with Christ on the Mountain where He was transfigured, both of them came to earth from two separate locations. When Moses died, his spirit was taken from his body and was carried into a special underground chamber where the souls of all righteous men were confined (Luke 16:22). Therefore, Moses, who died 1,500 years prior (Deut. 34:5-7), was temporarily brought up from this underground abode of the righteous dead for this one-time meeting with Christ. Elijah, on the other hand, had been transported upward to the third heaven in a heavenly chariot (2 Kings 2). For Elijah to appear, he had to descend from heaven to this mountain location. Luke 9:31 records their conversation with Christ, which centered on His coming death in Jerusalem. The Messiah's suffering was predicted by prophets such as David (Psalms 22) and Isaiah (Isaiah 53). Clearly, these two prophets had unique insight revealed to them that they shared with Christ during this strange meeting.

Understanding how prophetic events are seen and recorded thousands of years in advance helps explain the mystery of these two prophets' advanced knowledge of what was to come for Christ. A good example is with the Apostle John, who penned the lengthy visions recorded in the book of Revelation. From chapter four to chapter twenty-two, John's apocalyptic vision details a seven-sealed book, seven vials, and the seven trumpet judgments that have *not yet occurred*. It was over 1,900 years ago when John saw the details of what was coming as though it was actually happening at that moment.

Paul stated that "we see through a glass darkly," and we "know in part and we prophesy in part" (1 Corinthians 13:9-12). In verse 10, he says that when the one which is perfect comes (Christ), then what we know in part is done away with. The knowledge of only 'part' becomes knowledge of the 'whole.' The "whys" we had on earth will be answered along with mysteries we could not explain.

HEAVENLY KNOWLEDGE OF EARTHLY EVENTS

The spirit world having knowledge of future events is revealed in 2 Chronicles 18. King Ahab was seeking advanced knowledge about the outcome of an upcoming war. Over four hundred "false prophets" in Ahab's inner circle encouraged this evil king to engage in the war, falsely predicting a victorious outcome. However, one true prophet named Micaiah, from his musty dungeon, saw a vision of God's heavenly courtroom filled with angelic hosts, standing on the left and right side of God's throne. In this vision, the prophet indicates that God was preparing to "set up" Ahab to be slain during battle. The Almighty was discussing the method to convince Ahab to enter this final battle. The strategy was to persuade Ahab's "prophets" into believing Ahab would defeat this army, inspiring Ahab to engage in the conflict. There were dueling prophecies. Ahab's four hundred in-house prophets chirped in unison an outcome of victory, while one true man of God announced Ahab's emanate death. Ahab refused to heed the warning from Micaiah, choosing instead to follow the lies of his own palace prophets. The following day, after being shot with arrows, Ahab died (1 Kings 22:34-37).

Jesus spoke of God's will being done "on earth as it is in heaven" (Matt. 6:10). At times, major earthly decisions that affect nations or impact the kingdom of God are first strategized in the courts of heaven before they are enacted or embraced on the earth. Information and plans known to God and Christ can be passed on to angelic messengers whose assignment is to see that the decisions are set in motion on the earth.

King Nebuchadnezzar is an example. Due to his extreme arrogance, God allowed a seven-year mental breakdown to come upon this Babylonian leader. The book of Daniel indicates that God's judgment, called a "decree," was carried out by the "watchers," which were a special type of angels mentioned three times, only in Daniel (4:13, 17, 23). The Aramaic word for watcher is *iyr*, whose Aramaic root is *ir*, meaning "awake; watchful." One watcher angel was commissioned at a certain moment to cause the king's mind to snap, leading to a seven-year mental breakdown (Dan. 4:17). Heaven made the decree, and an angel performed the decree on earth.

Another illustration is when Christ was arrested in Gethsemane. Peter went into attack mode, slicing off the ear of the High Priest's servant. Jesus healed the man. Afterward, it was revealed that God had given Christ permission, if He chose, to call twelve legions of angels that would assist in His immediate release from death (Matt. 26:53). When was Christ made aware of this possibility? Another Gospel writer, Luke, reported that in the midst of Christ's agony, as His sweat became blood, "there appeared an angel from heaven, strengthening Him" (Luke 22:43). This sudden angelic appearance not only strengthened Christ to continue on, but he brought a powerful messenger, revealing a heavenly secret, that God had 12 legions (as many as 72,000) of His angelic forces on standby, should Christ not choose the route of suffering. A previously unknown backup plan prepared in heaven was made known on earth via the visitation of an angel.

WHAT DO DEPARTED SOULS SEE?

Can departed souls of men and women, now resting in the third heaven paradise, see the *good or the bad* we engage in on earth? Any *bad* acts or conduct by those living on earth, seen by a loved one in heaven, could cause sorrow or grief. The five senses and emotions do not cease at death but are linked with the human soul and emotions. On earth, many godly men and women experience extreme life challenges. Some single moms work two or three jobs to help raise their children. Others live with abusive companions or rebellious children whose negative actions strike heartache and pain. Heaven is a place of peace, and any negative or sad earthly information connected to your earthly family, revealed in paradise, would infect the perfection and eternal rest provided to those now with the Lord.

The key knowledge known in heaven would be the knowledge the individual soul had while *living* on earth. Earthy activities connected to *words and deeds* are recorded in heavenly books to be opened at the time of judgment. Christ said that "every idle word that men shall speak, they shall give an account of on the day of judgment" (Matt. 12:36). Paul said we would give an account of both the good and the bad (2 Cor. 5:10). Since both the "good" and the "bad" can surface at either of the judgments in heaven, a person must have earthly recall of words and actions from the past.

The only way to cancel *bad deeds* is by truly repenting of any sin while living on earth, turning, and forsaking any type of evil. Being cleansed by Christ's blood releases past sins, giving the person a new beginning as a new creation (2 Cor. 5:17). Through repentance, God said He would remember our sin no more, meaning that a repentant person will not answer for anything which has been blotted out and forgiven through the blood of Christ. It is written, Christ is "faithful and just to forgive us our sins and to cleanse us from all unrighteousness" (1 John 1:9). God expressed this to Israel, "I, even I, am he that blots out your transgressions for my own sake, and will not remember your sins" (Isaiah 43:25 NKJV). During the judgment of the righteous, rewards will be presented to the faithful. For those who did not run the race well, their judgment will conclude with a rebuke, and they will depart Christ's presence without any reward.

CAN A SOUL RETURN TO EARTH?

Can a departed soul presently in paradise ever return to earth before their resurrection that is set to occur at Christ's appearing? During four decades of ministry, I can recount numerous stories related to me from older Christians who are not "flaky" but are godly and known for their integrity. Their testimonies are trustworthy. They tell of seeing a loved one (specifically a husband) who had passed away, suddenly appearing to them. Three of these experiences stand out above the others.

Bea Ogle is one of the godliest women I have ever known. Since 1981, she has directed our Daughters of Rachel intercession ministry. I have personally known her since I was eighteen. Bea was married to Elroy Ogle for 64 years. Several years ago, Elroy, who was in his eighties, passed away, leaving her a widow with no biological children. Several weeks after Elroy's death, Bea was alone in her bedroom lying down trying to sleep. She felt an unusual presence enter the room. Suddenly, in full view, she saw Elroy dressed in a colorful shirt looking as he did when he was in his early thirties. He sat on the edge of the bed. She could *read his thoughts. It was* as clear as if they were carrying on a verbal conversation. He indicated his concern for the house and told her what she should do, and then suddenly, he vanished. She told me, "I was not asleep; neither was I dreaming." He had passed away before they could put a new roof on the house, and this was becoming a great concern for her.

A second incident told to me many years go occurred in Tuscumbia, Alabama. An older man, a strong Christian, told his wife that if he died before she did, he had left her a lot of cash hidden in the house. However, he never told her where this secret stash was. He suddenly passed away, and months later, she found herself needing additional income. She had searched through the draws and all other possible hiding places, finding no cash. After praying intently for God's help, one night, she awoke from a deep sleep and saw her husband standing at the closet near the bed. He opened the closet door and pointed to a stack of neatly folded blankets on the top shelf. He then pointed to the bottom blanket, smiled, then vanished.

When she came to herself, she turned on the light, opened the closet door, and pulled down several folded blankets. To her amazement, in the bottom blanket laid thousands of dollars that had been resting in the folds. She was stunned and amazed. She would have never thought of looking in that old blanket.

The third and most dramatic experience occurred when I was a small boy. My dad was pastoring in Big Stone Gap, Virginia. An older couple, the Coopers, attended our little church. When Mr. Copper died, his wife had no driver's license and lived miles away in Norton, but desired to continue attending our church. Her son from Tennessee spent days helping her move from Norton, Virginia, into a basement apartment located about fifty feet directly across from the church. Her son set a strict monthly budget, instructing her that she could no longer send her ten dollars a month to the Church of God World Missions, but must use that ten dollars on her groceries. From the time of their marriage, she and her husband never missed a month sending in their support for oversees soul wining. Her son told her that her "small" ten dollars each month "made no difference in winning souls," and "the missions department in Cleveland had plenty of money and didn't need hers." She rejected the idea, but her son demanded that she do this, especially since her income was now limited. She unwillingly complied with his wishes.

A few weeks later, when she was asleep, she was suddenly awakened by the sound of beautiful singing emitting from the small yard to the left outside of her apartment next to the church. A bright light was shining through her only bedroom window. Thinking she had over-slept, she was curious as to who was singing outside. Peeking out from behind the curtain of her bedroom window, she observed about forty or fifty people standing in several neatly formed rows on a small hill to her left. They stood between the apartment and the church, all dressed in white. They were singing a worship song. There was a man directing this "choir." His back was turned toward her. She could tell these individuals were from different nations. As they sang, suddenly, the man leading this choir, turned toward the window and it was her husband! He looked like he did when he was in his early thirties! When he saw her, he and the entire group began blowing her kisses. Immediately, the group of people began slowing floating upward, eventually disappearing into the atmosphere. As the light faded, the darkness returned. She then heard the Lord say, "These are the souls that were won with your ten dollars a month!"

She was so stunned. She immediately called my dad to get to her apartment quickly. Dad thought that perhaps she was having a heart attack. He dressed and swiftly ran the fifty-foot distance to her door, noticing that all the lights were on. As he walked in, she was sitting at her little table, writing out a ten-dollar check for world missions! She told Dad what she had seen and said, "Mail this world mission check to the mission's department and get it out of my house!" She knew this strange and exciting vision was a "sign" that years of giving to missions had won many souls, and it was both God's will and her husband's will that her giving must continue. Ten dollars was important for the work of God's kingdom.

THE SAME COMMON THREADS

These three incidents have several things in common. All three women were *widows* having no one that could personally provide for them. All three were experiencing a specific need that required some type of money or additional income. Did God allow their husbands to literally return from paradise, appearing to them, bringing comfort or needed information? Or was it a vision? Also, in each case, there was no verbal communication. Bea told me she could read Elroy's thoughts. With the second example, the late husband simply pointed to a location in the closet, and the third was a manifestation in which again, no words were spoken directly to the living person. Note that in all three instances, the husbands who had passed were in their eighties when they died, but all appeared to be in their early thirties. Also, these women were all married to their husbands for a long time, all over sixty years. An elderly widow often lives on limited income after her husband's departure, and this would be a concern to any loving and caring companion.

In each case, these three women of God believed the visual appearance of their companions was literal and not a hallucination nor a figment of their mind. Them being awake and fully alert made this a "real" experience. The question is, were their spirits and souls permitted to literally appear? Or was it more of a vision?

All three of these appearances *could be* considered a "vision." After Moses and Elijah appeared to Jesus, Christ told His three disciples to "tell no man the vision" (Matt. 17:9). By a Biblical measure, a vision is more than just a supernatural visible manifestation occurring late at night. Note how the women standing at Christ's tomb, who saw and spoke to the angels, called the experience a "vision" (see Luke 24:23). In these three cases, a "vision," in a broad sense, is a moment when the veil on the eyes is removed, and the visionary is enabled to see briefly into the spirit realm where the invisible is made visible. I have experienced numerous visions. In each case, the imagery I see is three dimensional with all five senses activated. I can feel the warmth, cold, feel the wind, and smell various fragrances.

Before a person writes off these incidents as unbiblical since they deal with a *departed* loved one, remember that Moses had been dead for 1,500 years. The Bible says twice that he "died" at the age of one hundred twenty (Deut. 34:5-7). However, Moses visibly appeared and was seen by Christ and three of His closest disciples. They gave additional information about Christ's future, as he and Elijah spoke of Christ's coming death in Jerusalem (see Luke 9:30-31). God did not resurrect Moses' body from the dirt for this encounter. It was the soul and spirit of Moses that appeared. This was called a "vision" (Matt. 17:9), and yet there was a conversation and a face-to-face encounter with Christ. I realize this is a rare and unusual occurrence. However, in the three previously mentioned cases, God could have permitted a vision, as was the case with Moses and Elijah. There are still mysteries connected with such experiences.

MISSIONS, MONEY, AND SOULS

In Mrs. Cooper's experience, once her husband's soul entered the heavenly paradise, he could have literally met the souls from various nations that were won to Christ through many years of their giving! These souls would be the "fruit that abounds to your account" that Paul alluded to in Philippians 4:17. Obviously, heaven records everyone's tithing and giving information, as indicated when the angel told Cornelius that his "Prayers and Alms (charitable giving) had come up before God" (Acts 10:4). The special rewards presented at judgment are given to soul-winners (1 Thess. 2:19). When Mrs. Cooper's son cut off the monthly mission's donation, the Lord knew how important this was for soul-winning to both her and to her husband. The only way Mrs. Cooper would experience the freedom to restore the ten dollars a month missions offering against her son's wishes was through this powerful, visible manifestation she experienced.

I have only had one specific incident of this type in my entire lifetime. I was very close to both my grandparents, John and Lucy Bava. Before his departure, Granddad began dreaming of seeing his mother and dad and a little brother that died in the 1930s. They were on a hill saying, "Johnny, it's time to come home." He would also see beautiful buildings in heaven and experience dreams of men that he once pastored who were now with the Lord in paradise. He passed away, leaving my grandmother, who moved to my hometown of Cleveland to live with her daughter Janet and be near my mother.

Before Grandmother died, her last conversation with me was of a dream she had where she saw Granddad (her husband) in heaven at a massive banquet hall where the marriage supper of the Lamb will occur. He told her there was much activity occurring in heaven as everyone was preparing for the marriage supper! In the dream, he showed her a beautiful table where the family would sit. Although in pain, she was elated with the experience. She went to be with the Lord about twenty-four hours later.

Shortly after her death, I was sleeping when I was suddenly wide awake with someone standing in the room about three feet from the foot of the bed to the right. To my surprise, it appeared to be my grandmother. She was not in a bodily form but was a three-dimensional soul-spirit form like a normal person. There was an intense brightness surrounding her. No words were ever said, but I could read her thoughts as though reading a script from a paper. She spoke of one event that dealt with my future that I have only shared with a few. Suddenly, she was no longer there, but that incident and that single thought remain with me to this day.

As a warning, the word of God teaches us not to *consult the dead*, which is what King Saul attempted to do when he met with the witch of Endor, hoping to bring Samuel's spirit from the underworld, an act forbidden by God (1 Sam. 28). However, in the above instances, not one person was attempting to make "contact with the other world" or asking God for some soul to appear. These "visions," however, are only possible in accordance with the sovereignty and will of God.

NO DESIRE TO RETURN

I have been asked if it were possible for someone in paradise to see their biological families, including their children and grandchildren. If they could, would they not have the desire to leave paradise and return back to earth to join their families? My answer is that where they now dwell is so beautiful, peaceful, and perfect that earth-living cannot compare to the *glory* they now experience. Also, the born-again (redeemed) family members living on earth will eventually either die or be alive at the return of Christ and rejoin their family in heaven. *We no longer wait on earth for them. They are waiting in heaven for us.*

During the Apostle Paul's traveling ministry, he was consistently hindered by a satanic angel who was creating opposition against him in almost every city where he ministered. As noted, in 2 Corinthians 11:23-27, Paul lists 22 distinct types of hindrances, including physical, natural, and spiritual opposition that made his ministry difficult. In his conversion experience, Christ warned Paul that he would "suffer great things for the Gospel" (Acts 9:16). After years of distress and weariness, Paul wrote that he preferred to "depart and be with Christ, which is far better." However, he understood, "to abide in the flesh is much needful for you" (Phil 1:23-24). Paul understood that he could die, enter the heavenly paradise, experience relief from all persecution and tribulation, or he could remain on earth, experience hindrances, and continue reaching the lost. He chose the latter.

Those who have encountered a near-death experience, in which they saw heaven or loved ones who are there, all indicated that the *perfect peace* of paradise was so intense that they had no desire to return to the earthly realm. However, in these near-death experiences, the individuals were given a life extension, returning to their bodies, further continuing their earthly assignment until their appointed time.

RECOGNIZING PEOPLE THAT WE NEVER KNEW

When I was a child, while preaching on heaven, ministers would say, "One day I will see Noah, Abraham, David, Paul, and the saints of old..." This is true. I am a very rational person whose mind ponders questions. My first thought was if I have never personally seen or met these patriarchs or Bible apostles, then how am I going to recognize them in heaven?

In the book of Revelation, a special angel was assigned to show John various events that would transpire after the end of the millennial reign of Christ. After John was shown the end of all things, including the new heaven, the new earth, and the New Jerusalem, he turned and fell down to worship the "angel" who had shown him many of these future events. Here is what followed:

> "Now I, John, saw and heard these things. And when I heard and saw, I fell down to worship before the feet of the angel who showed me these things. Then he said to me, "See that you do not do that. For I am your fellow servant, and of your brethren the prophets, and of those who keep the words of this book. Worship God." And he said to me, "Do not seal the words of the prophecy of this book, for the time is at hand."
>
> — REVELATION 22:8-10 (NKJV)

The entire time this heavenly messenger was unveiling the future to John, he assumed this person was an angel. However, this person called himself a "fellow servant" (of the Lord) and a "prophet." In Scripture, no angel was ever called a prophet, as this title is reserved for earthly men. With this messenger being a prophet from the past who now resided in heaven, we can assume this prophet had died, was now in heaven, and was revealing future revelations to John. Why did John not recognize this person if we will instantly recognize people in heaven?

The answer could potentially be found in the difference between the physical and the spiritual world. During the entire apocalyptic vision, John's body remained on the Island of Patmos. However, John said he was "in the Spirit on the Lord's day" (Rev. 1:10), meaning he saw into the mind and will of God. After seeing a vision of Christ (Rev. 1) and receiving messages to the seven churches (Rev. 2-3), John heard a voice like a trumpet. Immediately, he was standing *in the*

Spirit, in heaven, observing details from within God's eternal throne room. John had not died. His spirit had not exited his body. However, he participated in a living, full-color vision, revealing future events on earth and in heaven. On the Island of Patmos, John inscribed, with ink and parchment, various scenes that flowed like a movie. John's knowledge was limited to *earthy understanding,* and this is why he needed an angel to interpret the strange prophetic symbolism. At death, we have an unlimited ability to know as we were known (1 Cor. 13:12), and we will discern who others are. In the body, there are still limitations, and what is unknown must be made known through the Holy Spirit and through divine revelation.

One unique phrase stated by the heavenly messenger may hold a clue to this "angel's" identity. The angel told John "not to seal the book" (Rev. 22:10). After seeing a series of visions, one other prophet was told by an angel to "seal the book until the time of the end" (Dan. 12:4). Both Daniel and John's writings are Apocalyptic and parallel, often using the same symbolism, prophetic numbers, and words. Could Daniel have been the prophetic "angelic" messenger giving John the final words he penned in his vision? Daniel was a prophet. This made him a fellow servant of the Lord. Whoever this man was, he was not a prophet living on earth but had once been a servant of God and was now part of the heavenly assembly of saints dwelling in heaven.

How will we know people we have never met? There is a spiritual gift called the "word of knowledge" (1 Cor. 12:7-10). Through the Holy Spirit's gifting, a person is enabled to gain knowledge about people, places, events, and the future that they know nothing about in the natural realm.

Before Adam sinned, God brought him all the animals, instructing him to name each one. That would have been an impossible task without advanced levels of wisdom and knowledge. Christ operated using the word of knowledge as in the case where He saw (in the spirit)

Nathanael sitting under a tree (John 1:48). He also shocked a Samaritan woman when He revealed that she had relations with five different men and was now connecting with number six to whom she wasn't married (John 4:16-18).

Adam had incredible knowledge until sin suppressed it. Once we exit this body, which is surrounded by sinful humanity, there will be an amazing download of wisdom, knowledge, and understanding. Paul said, "Then shall I know even as I am known" (1 Cor. 13:12).

During the heavenly judgment, we will stand before God with the name we were known by on earth. Once rewards are given, one of the blessings for being an overcomer is that God will give us a "new name." It will be written on a white stone that represents a life of victory (Rev. 3:12). I suggest to you that this new name also represents a new beginning and is the removal of all of the former things.

A THIRD HEAVEN EXPERIENCE

Paul's third heaven experience was so dramatic for him that he discovered the reason he had a hindering spirit. It was there to prevent him from being exalted by what he had seen. The reason I tend to believe he had an out-of-body experience (where Paul's spirit temporarily departed from his body) is the fact that he saw and visited paradise while in the third heaven. Paradise is the abode for the spirits of the dead. Although their body is deceased on earth, they continue to live with all their former earthly abilities in the heavenly paradise. If Paul was dead, this heavenly journey could have occurred in Lystra. This is where Paul was stoned and left for dead, but the disciples prayed for him, and he was raised from death. The amazing miracle is that the following day, after being stoned and left for dead, he continued on a journey to a new ministry location (Acts 14:19-20).

Mankind's technology has been unable to tap into the third heaven dimension because the distance from the earth to the eternal city of God is too far to be reached by human methods. The third heaven can only be seen by three methods: in a spiritual dream, in a vision, or in an actual experience similar to what Paul alluded to when he spoke about the human spirit being transported at the speed of thought to the third heaven.

There is a reason the heavens are divided. When God created the heavens and the earth, the earth was made for man, and heaven was created for the spirit world. After the expulsion of Satan and the fallen angels (which occurred before the creation of man), hell was created for the devil and his angels (Matt. 25:41).

Heaven has been given to men who have an eternal spirit, to God who controls the third heaven, and to a kingdom of darkness who travels at the speed of thought and has dominion in the second heaven. Because of the fall of man, Satan has total access (at this time) to the first heaven. This is clear when we read that Satan is the "prince of the power of the air." Greek scholars point out that the word here for air in Greek refers to the area from the ground on earth, to the upper atmosphere where the clouds are.

THE PARADISE SECTION

Thousands of sermons and books have been written about heaven. We have sermonized heavenly realities, and at times, have not painted a full picture of what the Bible *actually* teaches. We hear:

- We will live forever in heaven

- We will live in a mansion with God in heaven

- We will rest eternally from our work

As far as manual labor, those entering paradise are commanded to "rest." They have ceased from their labors.

It is clear that there are spiritual veils or coverings that hide the invisible world from the visible. Adam and Eve were unaware they were naked until after they ate from the tree of knowledge. We read that the moment they ate, "the eyes of both of them were opened" (Gen. 3:7). Their physical condition was hidden from them until something lifted from their eyes.

I am reminded of one of Elisha's stories. One day he awoke to his camp being surround by an enemy army. He stood on a hill and saw the that Syrian Army had surrounded them and their mountain in a secret military maneuver because they were intent on capturing him. The prophet was unmoved while his servant was nearly having a breakdown. Elisha told his servant that he did not see what Elisha was seeing. The prophet prayed, "Lord, open his eyes that he may see. And the Lord opened the eyes of the young man" (2 Kings 6:17). Again, some type of covering was removed, and the servant saw an army of angels and chariots protecting them. There are natural and spiritual eyes and natural and spiritual ears.

Without the human eyes being veiled keeping hidden the invisible world, it is possible that men and women could not function effectively. They could be continually frozen with fear, if they saw both angels flying and ministering or if they tapped into the demonic world of evil spirits surrounding evil people or strategizing against the righteous. In Scripture, when men saw angels, the angelic messenger often told the person to fear not. In Job, Eliphaz spoke of sleeping at night and fear coming upon him when a spirit passed before his face, and the hair of his flesh stood up (Job 4:15). The covering that prevents us from seeing the invisible world is for our own protection. However, once the spirit is outside of the body, all spirits of all forms can be seen by the person who is passing.

On earth, the Holy Spirit makes known the will of God as it has been planned in heaven. Angels are heavenly agents assigned to bring important information, especially that prophetic in nature, to the earth, revealing future events to prophets and prophetic centered believers. God's written word, the Holy Bible, is our main source in understanding both God's present and future will. We pray God's will be done on earth as it is in heaven. Information is needed on earth as in heaven. The information we have on earth that comes from heaven is by the Word of God and the Holy Spirit, who show us things to come.

CHAPTER THREE

HOW IS TIME
COUNTED IN HEAVEN?

T ime is an earth feature that began its "official" count the day Adam was created in Eden. Time always moves forward yet recycles every 365.25 days. The sun determines the day, the moon the month, and the circuit of the earth's movement around the sun constitutes the years. God's calendar is cosmic and in cyclical-time flows, passing through four seasons: spring, summer, fall, and winter. The four seasons during the year also signal planting and harvest cycles. Time was intended for men living on earth but is not necessary for the spirit world.

This can be seen in the fact that God dwells in three ages: ages past, this present age, and the ages to come. The ages past cannot be dated as no one knows when the "beginning" actually was (Gen. 1:1). Christians date earth-time from the creation of Adam, which, according to Biblical chronology, was slightly over 6,000 years ago. Some Christian scientists hold a view that creation was progressive, a gradual process taking millions of years. Evolutionists take extreme and unfounded liberty in marking the earth as billions of years old and giving imaginary dates to pieces of petrified bone and fossils.

From the Biblical view, time can be counted by three different methods: sabbatical cycles, jubilee cycles, and God-ordained covenants. Every seventh day, called the Sabbath, is set aside for men and animals to rest (Exod. 16:23-29). The Hebrews were to mark every seventh year as a Shmita cycle, in which Israel refrained from agricultural labor and the land lay fallow (unplowed) for one year (Exod. 23:10-11). Seven Shmita cycles (seven years times seven years) or every forty-nine years, a silver trumpet sounded on the Day of Atonement signifying the year of Jubilee, which was not only a year of national freedom and release, but a period set aside for debt cancellation, a recovery of family property, and a call for freedom allowing Hebrew slaves to return home to their families (Lev. 25).

Throughout the centuries, various writers have attempted to place Israel's major prophetic and national events in seven-year cycles. One non-canonical book, the Book of Jubilees, dated between 100 to 150 B.C., written by an unknown source, attempts to place all of Israel's major events, from the fall of Adam through Israel's early Biblical history including the Maccabean revolt, into a set pattern of sevens where major events fall on the *Jubilee years*. While many of Israel's significant events can be traced to cyclical patterns, others transpired on a more random scale.

Lastly, God marks time by covenants. A theologically controversial, yet extremely interesting verse in Matthew gives credence to a covenant counting theory. Matthew lists the genealogical record of Christ, beginning with Abraham and concluding with Joseph and Mary who were of the house of David (Matt. 1:1-16). In Matthew 1:17, we read a summary:

> "So all the generations from Abraham to David are fourteen generations; and from David until the carrying away into Babylon are fourteen generations; and from the carrying away into Babylon unto Christ are fourteen generations."

Abraham was the first man to enter a blood covenant with God through circumcision (Gen. 17:11). Abraham was also the father of the faith (Rom. 4:1). Moving forward from Abraham fourteen generations, David enters the picture as God chose a Davidic dynasty, establishing covenants with him, promising to give his male descendants a throne in Jerusalem. Fourteen generations from David, Israel broke their land covenant by not honoring the jubilee cycles and were punished as God permitted the Jews to experience captivity for seventy years as exiles in Babylon. Counting fourteen generations from Babylon, the next and final covenant introduced is the new covenant of redemption initiated through Jesus Christ. Each situation involved a chosen person entering a new covenant with God, as in the case with Babylon, Israel broke the land covenant through disobedience. The number fourteen (generations) separated the various covenants or breaking of the covenant. This sets a clear pattern that God marks time in relation to covenants.

All three of these cycles were given to the righteous on earth to mark lifetimes, prophetic events, and covenants. Even the seven major Torah festivals of Israel were to be celebrated in a repetitive manner, on the same month and same day each year. *Time was needed on earth to know the set time of these special seasons, sabbaticals, and prophetic events.*

TIME IN THE LAND OF NO TIME

Heaven was created in the beginning (Gen. 1:1), and no living person knows when the actual "beginning" was. This is called "eternity past," meaning a timeless past that is marked by mysterious events. The celestial heaven is a vast open space dotted with trillions of stars. The time spent to create the heavens is unknown. God spoke "light" on the first day (Gen 1:3). God created the sun, moon, and stars on the fourth day (Gen. 1:14-19). Note that the heavens and earth were created prior to the announcement of the "light." This makes the actual beginning (Gen. 1:1) of an unknown time frame.

When God entered the earth-zone, the entire creative process, including the forming of man, was performed in six days. In Hebrew, the word for *day* is *yom* and refers to a twenty-four-hour period called a day. When sin entered man's domain, God placed all humans on a timeline—birth to death. There is a set date with a beginning called "birth" and a set "appointed" time for life to end called "death" (Heb. 9:27). Once man's earth-time ceases, then the eternal spirit within each person will enter one of two never-ending regions: heaven or hell, both were created and exist in the "no time zone."

All spirits, including God, Christ, the Holy Spirit, the holy angels, Satan, his evil spirits, and fallen angels are presently dwelling in the timeless realm. When the Bible says, "For the devil has come down to you, having great wrath, because he knows that he has a short time" (Rev. 12:12 NKJV), it refers to his rule over mankind on earth coming to an end, as God has placed a time limitation on him. Satan's future confinement has been set for one thousand years, and since the bottomless pit is located under the *earth* (earth-time), this set time is a literal thousand years (Rev. 20:2). After the thousand years confinement and following the Great White Throne judgment, Satan will be cast into the Lake of Fire forever and ever, meaning for *eternity,* which is a never-ending time (Rev. 20:10). Thus, all spirit forms without a physical body now dwell, in some manner, in a timeless zone. However, when any spirit sent from either God or Satan enters and operates on earth, they are aware of and become subject to cosmic time—minutes, days, weeks, months, and years.

When Daniel was fasting and praying for God to give him an understanding of a prophetic mystery, once entering the earth's atmosphere, the angel sent by God was hindered. The angel later informed Daniel that he had been restrained by a demonic prince spirit (called the prince of Persia) for twenty-one days (Dan. 10). In Daniel 11:1, the angel whose ministry on earth dealt with kings and princes spoke of the "first-year" of King Darius' rule. The angel left heaven, the land of eternity, and entered the earth's time zone. We see here that all angelic messengers or satanic spirits are placed on a platform of measurable time.

An interesting verse in 2 Peter informs us that "one day with the Lord is as a thousand years and a thousand years is as one day" (2 Pet. 3:8). In context, Peter is writing about the return of the Lord, and reminding the church that God is faithful to fulfill His promise of Christ returning for us, even though it might be a long time in the future. Peter notes that God views time differently than us. For us, a thousand years is a long, long time, yet to God, it seems like one day.

In the book of Revelation, there are set times that cannot be altered during the earth's final seven-year prophetic cycle (the tribulation) that climaxes with Christ's return. One such predetermined time is 1,260 days, or forty-two months (Rev. 11:3; 12:6; 13:5). When the seven-year tribulation arrives (Dan. 9:27), specific set times will trigger the earth's clock to tick down, and when the final second arrives, Satan and the Antichrist's time will be up. God then responds by releasing the armies of heaven, mighty angels, and the saints of all ages, led by Christ Himself, back to earth to defeat the world's warring armies, to bind Satan, and to set up the Messiah's kingdom! Satan's earthly control is on a time limit!

WHAT DO THE DEAD KNOW PROPHETICALLY?

I believe the souls of the dead dwelling in paradise are unaware of the earth's timeclock. However, the righteous souls of men and women will be the first alerted to the fact that Christ is preparing to return to the earth for the resurrection of the dead and the "gathering together" of the living saints also known as the "Rapture" (2 Thess. 2:1). In preparation for this massive number of resurrected and living saints to arrive, and considering the preparations for the Bema (Rev. 11:18) and the Marriage Supper of the Lamb (Rev. 19:7-9), the activity occurring in heaven *to prepare for these events* is known in heaven. Thus, the souls of the righteous are aware that the major end-time events of which the prophets spoke will soon occur.

One of the most dramatic stories revealing what is occurring in paradise was related to me by a pastor friend, Ron Stewart, whom I interviewed on television. He shared how years ago, he had experienced severe chest pains. The doctors discovered a dangerous staff infection that had occurred as a result of the wires in his pacemaker deteriorating and going into his heart. He began taking antibiotics for an extended time, only to discover that his organs were being infected. He was also informed that he had three heart blockages. Without surgery, he would die, and with surgery, he had a twenty percent chance of living. He chose surgery at the Texas Medical Center in the Dallas area.

During surgery, while his heart was out of his chest, he was suddenly "awake." Looking to his right, he spotted a large angel dressed in white that appeared about eight-feet tall. This angel took his spirit by the hand and lifted his spirit out of his body. He was able to see the doctors working on him. Within seconds, he was flying fast through the upper realm of space when he was suddenly standing with the angel in the beautiful courtyard of a big arena. In the distance, sitting at a table were his grandmother, his aunt, and a child that had died fifteen years prior. His aunt was talking to a man and pointing to a beautiful mansion and saying how surprised she was that this was hers. He asked the angel who the man was. The angel replied, "He was a man named Anderson who, on earth, was a mentor to her." After Ron was strengthened and gave his testimony on YouTube, a man contacted him, telling him he knew who Anderson was. Years ago, the caller had attended Bible School with Ron's Aunt. Mr. Anderson was the head of the school and spent time mentoring and teaching her. Mr. Anderson had died about a year prior to Ron's heavenly encounter.

The angel then led Ron to another arena similar to a stadium, and from the middle of the arena, he looked around and could see layers of beautiful mansions going upward inside this amazing celestial structure. Some were double-decked, and the outside was covered with beautiful gemstones. What we would use on earth as cement was actually gold. The predominant color was a sapphire blue, which is the same color Ezekiel described as the throne of God (see Ezek. 10:1). While in this arena, he also saw his wife's grandmother dancing with a girl that looked about ten years old. He asked the angel, "Who is that girl?" The angel replied, "That is her child, a girl she had that was stillborn." Ron had never heard that she had a still-born child. When he returned and was able to speak to his wife, she called her mother and asked her about *her mother* having a baby girl. Ron's mother-in-law said, "It is true. I remember when I was a little girl, Mom gave birth to a little girl that was still-born, but we never talked about it!" Ron had seen the little girl in paradise with her mother.

In paradise, after leaving the area of the gem-studded mansions, Ron was immediately directed by the angel to a third and very fascinating area. In this part, he saw countless stunning stables, and in the open fields were tens of thousands of beautiful and very large strong horses. Each had a unique breastplate covering, with unusual looking writing embedded on each breastplate. He noticed one white stallion with a bright silver breastplate also engraved with the same letters. It was in a language he could not understand. He asked the angel, "What does that say?" The angel replied, "In your language, it says 'Faithful and True.'" The reference to the white horse and the words "faithful and true" are found in Revelation 19:11. The other horses were draped in colors of crimson and gold.

There were some with riders and one man, who was like a military general, was giving orders. When this man spoke, the horses would raise from the ground and some would form a circle. Ron asked the angel, "What are they doing?" The angel replied, "On earth you would call these military maneuvers. They are preparing for war." There were other horses that had no riders. When the angel was asked why there were no riders on these, he replied, "Their riders have not yet arrived." I asked Ron in the interview if he believed these were the horses referred to in Revelation 19 where the armies of heaven would ride to earth during the battle of Armageddon. He replied that he did believe this was what he saw.

The last thing he saw before returning to his body that was lying in the hospital was another very large room where there was a man instructing a group of people. When asked what he was teaching, the angel said, "He is teaching young children and also people who received Christ at an older age on earth, he is instructing them about worship." Ron understood that some children die before they can ever experience the act of worship, and some older people are converted to Christ at such an older age, they die, never experiencing true worship on earth. At that moment, the angel said, "You are not staying, you are only visiting." He began looking around to see other people that he knew had died in the faith and did not see them. The angel's last words were, "Just because you do not see them does not mean they are not here." Ron returned to his body that was in a coma. He eventually woke up and recovered to tell this story. Notice that there are preparations being made for what is to come in the future, and because he was not a permanent resident in paradise as of yet, his knowledge was limited to only what was revealed to him by the angel, or what he knew on earth, such as the people he had known.

WHEN THE DEAD REUNITE WITH THEIR BODIES

When Christ prepares to return for the rapture, the souls of the righteous dead, beginning with those who died since the days of Christ's resurrection, will descend from heaven and be rejoined in a new glorified body, at the return of Christ for the church. Paul saw this and wrote in 1 Thessalonians 4:13-14:

> "But I would not have you to be ignorant, brethren, concerning them which are asleep, that ye sorrow not, even as others which have no hope. For if we believe that Jesus died and rose again, even so them also which sleep in Jesus will God bring with him."
>
> — 1 Thessalonians 4:13-14

At this resurrection, Christ is returning in the "air," and we who are living will be transformed from mortal to immortal, immediately being "caught up in the clouds to meet the Lord in the air" (1 Thess. 4:17). How can Christ raise a dead body that has long turned to dust on the earth, and at the same time, bring those who "sleep" (a metaphor for those who are dead) "with Him" when He descends from heaven (1 Thess. 4:16)? Part of this mystery is that it involves two locations.

The physical body of a person may have returned to dust, but their soul and spirit have been fully aware, continuing to live, resting in the third heaven paradise. Christ will call from heaven to these souls who will immediately join Him in the air in the clouds. Then a mystery will unfold as the ashes and dust will arise, and a new body will be formed around the spirit. This body will never again experience death. Daniel saw the resurrection and wrote:

> "And many of them that sleep in the dust of the earth shall awake, some to everlasting life, and some to shame and everlasting contempt."
>
> — Daniel 12:2

Those now dwelling in the third heaven paradise will be the first alerted at the moment of their earthly resurrection, as this is when they will receive a new, glorified body. When all believers have received their new, glorified bodies, they will have entered the no time zone. From that point, they will live forever in what is called "eternity." In Isaiah 57:15, the prophet wrote that the "high and lofty One (God) inhabits eternity." The word eternity is a never-ending duration and is also linked with the words, eternal (found 45 times in the New Testament), everlasting (found 26 times in the New Testament), and a phrase in Ephesians 3:21, "world without end."

CHAPTER FOUR

WHAT TYPE OF BODY DO THE DEPARTED NOW HAVE?

Throughout religious history, various beliefs have emerged related to what occurs when a human being expires. The world's three monotheistic religions are Christianity, Islam, and Judaism. These three religions all believe in an afterlife, including a future resurrection followed by a judgment. All who have lived will be judged by God Himself.

In the Christian faith, there are numerous denominations, many of which hold the same fundamental, foundational beliefs. One area of difference, however, is what occurs to the soul and spirit *of a person after they die.* Some teach that at death, the soul and spirit remain in the corpse where the soul enters a state of "sleep." This belief teaches that the soul resides in the same location as the person's body. This sleeping soul "rests" at this location until the day Christ resurrects the dead. This theory is called the doctrine of soul sleep.

Many others, including myself, believe that at death, both the righteous and unrighteous soul and spirit departs the physical body and is immediately transported to a specific location where the person's spirit awaits the resurrection. Remember, the resurrection is something that occurs to both the righteous and the unrighteous. For the righteous, the temporary abode of the departed is called paradise and is located in the third heaven (2 Cor. 12:1-4). For the unrighteous, the holding chamber, until the Great White Throne judgment, is identified as hell in both the Old and New Testaments (Isa. 5:14; Rev. 20:1-14). Hell is mentioned 54 times throughout the Bible and is always "down." This massive underworld chamber is both darkness and fire (Mark. 9:22-49).

Both the righteous and unrighteous dead will be raised from their opposing holding places. They will be judged in two different settings at two different heavenly judgments. The righteous will stand at the Judgment Seat of Christ called, in Greek, the "Bema" (Rom. 14:10). This group will be raised from the dead at the return of Christ when He appears in the air to catch away the living saints (1 Thess. 4:16-17). The unrighteous will be judged at the Great White Throne judgment at the conclusion of the thousand-year reign of Christ (Rev. 20:11-15).

When Christ returns, the righteous who have died since the time of Christ (called the "dead in Christ"— 1 Thess. 4:16) will be given an incorruptible new body that will live eternally and never experience death again. The unrighteous are different. Their souls and spirits are what will be judged, and they will not be given a new glorified body like the righteous. John said it this way, "Death and hell delivered up the dead that were in them." When these souls are found guilty, they are condemned to the "Lake of Fire," and this is called the second death. Their "first death" was when they physically died on earth and were confined in hell, and the "second death" is when they are eternally separated from God in the Lake of Fire (Rev. 20:14-15).

A resurrected body is an actual "body" with the same form and features of the previous earthly body. For some reason, people imagine that a departed human spirit is more like a beam of bright light, a fog or vapor, or a sort of see-through, semi-transparent hologram that has no bones, and certainly, no flesh, since "flesh and blood cannot inherit the kingdom" (1 Cor. 15:50). This idea of light or vapor is incorrect as

Christ, in a resurrected body, wore clothes, ate with His disciples, and was touched by Thomas.

THE TALE OF TWO RESURRECTIONS

Two individuals in the New Testament, Lazarus and Christ, were resurrected in their earthly bodies *prior to their flesh deteriorating.* Devout Jews bury individuals the same day they die, or if death occurs at night, burial is the following morning. Religious Jews do not embalm the dead the way the Egyptians did. They allow the blood to remain in the body. Lazarus's body still had blood, but Christ's blood was all poured out from His body through the crucifixion. Christ was in the tomb for three days and nights, and Lazarus was raised on the fourth day. The difference is, having no blood, the body of Christ was perfectly preserved. Peter noted that Christ "did not see corruption" (Acts 2:27), speaking of Christ's body not deteriorating in the tomb. Christ's body was smeared with one hundred pounds of spices and wrapped in linen, which again preserved Him for His bodily resurrection (John 19:39-40). He arose with a flesh and bone body, proven when He told Thomas to "touch Him" as a "spirit hath not flesh and bones" (Luke 24:39). It was necessary for Christ's body to be raised with the crucifixion wounds remaining visible in His hands, feet, and His side. Thomas saw and touched Christ's nail wounds and His side (John 20:27-28). The prophet Zechariah indicates that when the Messiah (Christ) returns to earth, men will see His wounds in His hands (see Zechariah 13:6). Christ's wounds are the visible evidence that He is the Messiah and has fulfilled the Messianic prophecies (see Psalms 22:1-8).

Before Lazarus was raised, those at the tomb warned, "By now he stinks," referring to his body beginning to corrupt, since his blood remained in his body (John 11:39). The body of Lazarus was also wrapped in linen, and when he was raised, men removed the grave clothes as his body did not pass through the linen covering him. Christ's body, however, appears to have completely passed through the grave clothes as His resurrected body slipped through the linen, leaving the grave clothes on the stone slab (John 20:7).

These points are significant. Lazarus would die again in the future. Christ would never die again. Lazarus was raised in his exact physical body with blood, and Christ was also raised in His own body free from blood. Christ was raised never to die again, which indicates His bodily form was not in a corruptible state but was raised in an *incorruptible* state. After Lazarus was raised, he functioned as any normal man, returning to human limitations, until his death. Christ, however, was able to travel long distances, sometimes without walking. On the road to Emmaus, after speaking with two men, He suddenly vanished from their sight (Luke 24:31). Later, these same two men were in Jerusalem relating the amazing conversation they had with Christ when suddenly, Christ appeared to them passing through a closed door (Luke 24:36). One moment He *disappeared*, and another moment He *reappeared* in a different location. Christ, in His new body, moved at the speed of thought. Angels who are spirits are also enabled to move at the speed of thought, appearing and disappearing at will.

This appearing and disappearing, at first, caused the disciples to believe they were seeing the "spirit" of Christ and not His actual body, as it is written, "They were terrified and afraid and supposed they had seen a spirit" (Luke 24:37). Knowing their confusion, this was when Christ informed them that His body consisted of flesh and bones (Luke 24:39).

The ability of Christ to transport Himself like an angel, with a body of *flesh and bones,* is somewhat of a mystery. The same is true with the mystery of how angels who are spirits (Psa. 104:4), can alter their spirit bodies and appear in the form of human men. The two men who appeared to Abraham in his tent, and afterward warned Lot at

Sodom, were actually angels who did not appear in their angelic mode but as human men. The wicked men of Sodom asked Lot to bring them out into the streets so they could have physical relations with them (Gen. 18 - 19). The body of Lazarus was restored later to die. However, the body of Christ was raised to live forever.

A RESURRECTED BODY

In 1 Corinthians 15, Paul explains to the church the mystery of the resurrection. A question was asked. How can there be a resurrection of a person who has died, and their body returned back to *dust*? Paul used the simple analogy of a seed planted in the ground. The seed represents a person who is placed in the earth at death. The seed must actually die or deteriorate in the earth before the living seed concealed within the shell of the buried seed is released from its concealment, bringing forth a living plant (1 Cor. 15:35-37). He further explains that the body is sown at death in corruption but will be raised from death in incorruption. The word *corruption* in Greek refers to the process of the body decaying. The word *incorruption* is used four times in the English translation, all in 1 Corinthians 15 (verses 42, 50, 53, and 54), and alludes to immortality or having an unending existence.

Each human consists of a physical body, and inside that body resides a soul and a spirit (1 Thess. 5:23). The next resurrection, scheduled by God, is the resurrection of the "Dead in Christ," meaning the resurrection of those who died with a redemptive covenant through the Lord Jesus Christ! At the return of Christ (called the Rapture), the dead in Christ rise first, and the living will meet them in the air (1 Thess. 4:16-17). The common New Testament Greek word for resurrection is *anastasis*, which means "to cause to stand; to raise up," and can also mean "to rise up out of a deep sleep." With the New Testament being written in the Koine (common) Greek language, this meaning may be why some New Testament writers spoke about the death of a believer by saying they are "asleep" (1 Cor. 15:6, 18; 1 Thess. 4:13, 15). The Greek word *koimao* can allude to *being put to sleep*, and figuratively *to decease*. Paul was not stating that at death, a believer's soul was asleep in the body. He was using a word that refers to someone being put to sleep and *comparing it* to a believer who closes their eyes at death.

The resurrection is actually a *rebirthing of something that previously existed*. When Christ was resurrected, a theological question arose as to why Mary, who was continually with Him during His ministry, did not recognize Him. The women closest to Christ refused to flee the crucifixion as did ten of Christ's original disciples. The women remained in the crowd at the foot of the cross. For three days, Christ was entombed in a limestone cavern-like sepulcher behind a round rolling stone weighing an estimated two tons. He arose early in the morning and was spotted by Mary, who thought He was the gardener, as the tomb was located in the garden of the wealthy Joseph of Arimathea (John 19:38-42), whom church tradition teaches was a wealthy tin trader.

Mary did not recognize Christ's physical appearance. However, His voice was the same. When He said, "Mary," she knew the sound of His voice. This inability to visually know it was Christ may have been because it was still dark, or the type of clothing Christ wore was different, but His voice had never changed.

THE SPIRITUAL BODY

Paul wrote:

> "So also is the resurrection of the dead. It is sown in corruption;
> it is raised in incorruption: It is sown in dishonor; it is raised
> in glory: it is sown in weakness; it is raised in power: it is sown
> a natural body; it is raised a spiritual body. There is a natural
> body, and there is a spiritual body."
>
> — 1 CORINTHIANS 15:42-44

We all presently have a natural body, but what is a spiritual body?
The natural body gains its lifeforce through the blood. It pumps from
the heart, flows through the arteries, and veins, into all the blood ves-
sels and vital organs. The "life of the flesh is in the blood" (Lev. 17:11).
Notice the life (soul) is not just the blood but is *in* the blood. There are
white and red cells *in* the blood. The blood carries oxygen. One blood
test can reveal every disease working within the body.

The "life" residing within the redeemed human spirit is the eternal
life or never-ending life that God imparts once the body is resurrected from the flesh (all natural) to completely spiritual. The natural
body survives in a world filled with limitations. Time moves forward,
including the aging process where every fleshy body wrinkles, develops
skin sags, and everyone gets old.

A spirit body does *not have the limitations* of a natural body. The
flesh needs rest, but the spiritual body does not. Both God and angels
are "spirits," and neither require sleep (Psa. 121:4). During the Exodos
in the wilderness, the natural bodies of the people required manna
or literal bread from heaven (Psa. 78:24). The spiritual body feeds on
heavenly manna, which is the Word of God, as man "shall live by
every word from God" (Matt. 4:4). Man's natural limitations include
the methods used when traveling distances, but the spiritual body can

transport with unlimited speed and is not restrained by walls, doors, or physical obstacles.

There are natural senses and spiritual senses. We all have ears. However, there are inner spiritual ears that can discern the voice of God and the Holy Spirit (Rev. 2:7). We all have eyes, but our spiritual eyes are linked with the ability to comprehend spiritual truth (Eph. 1:18). In Scripture, when men saw angels in their spirit form, it required some type of veil or covering on their eyes to be removed, as was the case when Elisha prayed that his servant's eyes would be opened to see the heavenly horses and chariots of fire protecting them (2 Kings 6:14-17).

Once we move outside of the human sphere, the intensity of the five senses is multiplied at a higher level, including colors, smells, and sounds, since the spiritual realm exists on a higher dimension.

All human limitations cease when a believer receives a new spiritual body. This is evident as God, who is a Spirit (John 4:24) and who dwells in the third heaven, can see each person on earth without using any form of viewing technology or telescopes. Prayers are spoken on earth and are heard immediately in the ears of Christ and the Father. The "touch" of God is released from heaven and is immediately felt on earth through the Holy Spirit. In Acts, on the Day of Pentecost, there was a "sound from heaven," which was overheard by worshippers on earth (Acts 2:1-4).

Using human ingenuity, men on earth have created powerful telescopes and computers that bring scenes from the edge of the galaxy back to earth. NASA can send signals toward planets and to the Mars rover to take pictures that are processed and sent to large screens for viewing. Indeed, the spirit realm has a far more advanced process of viewing, hearing, and traveling than any of us can comprehend.

SUPERNATURAL TRANSPORTATION

The invisible realm of angels, demons, God, and Satan is as real as the three-dimensional world we can see on a daily basis. Sound travels at a distance of 330 miles per second while light travels at 186,000 miles per second. Thus, if sound is wrapped in light, then the sound molecules should move within the path of light. The spirit world moves faster than light, enabling all spirit-beings to reduce the time distances and move faster than thought.

When Christ was baptized in water, a "voice from heaven" said, "This is my beloved son in whom I am well pleased" (Matt. 3:17). On a second occasion, God spoke from heaven in a voice heard publicly in which He said, "I have glorified it (my name) and will glorify it again" (John 12:28). The voice came from above as indicated when some thought it was the sound of *thunder* (John 12:29). God's voice can be heard at any time or any place as He is omnipresent, as He speaks from heaven, His voice can be heard on the earth.

When Daniel was praying from his apartment in Babylon, his answer was hindered for three weeks. However, when a heavenly messenger broke through the demonic barrier in the upper heavenly realm, Daniel was informed that his prayer had been heard "the first day he prayed," meaning God heard his words twenty-one days prior to this angelic visitation (see Daniel 10).

Distances can be compressed in the world of spirits and are also insignificant when the human spirit is outside of the body. As previously stated, Paul was stoned in Lystra and was left for dead (Acts 14:19; 2 Cor. 11:25). He later spoke of being "caught up into the third heaven," and was uncertain if he was "in or out of his body," meaning he was uncertain if his experience was a vision or if he actually died and went to paradise and returned.

If his spirit and soul departed temporarily from his physical body, then Paul instantly and supernaturally traveled from earth to the third heaven in order to see and experience what he did.

There are several veiled references to supernatural transportation within the scriptures. On one occasion, Christ was on a high mountain praying, and He perceived that the disciples were in danger in the middle of the sea. Having been on the Galilee mountains and knowing the distance from the mountain to the middle of the lake, it would have required Christ about an hour to walk down the mountain and walk on water to the disciple's boat. Yet, when Jesus perceived their trouble, He was immediately at the boat and calmed their storm. This event required some type of supernatural transportation from one location to another within a very short amount of time.

On another occasion, Christ and the disciples were riding a boat from one side of the lake to the other. After calming a storm which unfolded in the middle of their journey, they were immediately on the other side. The lake, at times, was seven miles wide. Using logic, if the storm ceased in the middle of the sea and immediately, the boat was on the other side, the boat and its crew were transported two to three miles in a brief time!

One amazing example is when Phillip was ministering in Samaria, and the Lord told Him to journey to Gaza and minister to an Ethiopian reading the scrolls of the prophets but lacked understanding. Phillip arrived, joining the chariot, expounding on the scripture then baptizing the man in water. Immediately, the Spirit of God caught Phillip up, transporting him back to Samaria to complete the revival.

There are two methods of "spirit travel." The first is through a spiritual vision in which you remain "in the body," but you are "caught up" into another dimension, including heaven itself and God allows you to see in the Spirit specific details of hidden or mysterious people, places, angels or the operation of the spirit world. "Paul spoke of being, "Out of the body," which is the second form of supernatural transportation. Out of body is when the spirit is temporarily released from the confines of the body, but not permanently like when death occurs, as the spirit returns to the physical body.

When John was imprisoned on the Island of Patmos, he was "in the Spirit on the Lord's day" (Rev. 1:10). He began receiving an amazing vision of Christ and eventually heard a trumpet, and a voice saying, "come up here," and immediately he was standing in the heavenly throne room of God. Most scholars do not believe his spirit left his body but that his spiritual eyes were open to the spirit world, and he was given the ability to see into three realms at once — what was in heaven, what was on earth, and what was under the earth.

It is humanly impossible to will your spirit to travel back and forth from some heavenly realm to earth. This is why many heavenly visitations are visions which enable a person's spiritual eyes to be opened to see the invisible.

I have met individuals who suffered from a heart attack, requiring them to be revived through the use of electrical shock paddles. Some describe pain, passing out, and total blackness until they were revived. Others tell of severe pain, passing out, and seeing what they describe as a heavenly paradise or a dark chamber lit with fire.

Outside of the body, both vision and hearing are enlarged and more sensitive, as the earthly limitations of time and space are removed! This is why we should not doubt the literal interpretation of Lazarus and the rich man in hell.

Our natural bodies are restricted by earthly limitations. Human infirmities and all forms of disease are part of living in a natural body. Our new resurrected bodies will be exempt from any and all sickness or infirmities. Any type of physical handicaps that cause a person to be confined in a wheelchair will end at death, and never again will the spirit of a righteous soul be limited by any physical handicaps.

Children who never walked will walk. They will even run! Any missing limbs will be restored and made whole.

In the New Testament, Christ cured a man born blind whose occupation was begging for a living (Luke 18:35-43). I have imagined what he felt when he saw the beauty of creation and the faces of his family for the first time. Imagine if you've never seen anything ever before. Take a person who was born blind and served Christ. Imagine their moment of death when their spirit-eyes are immediately opened, and the first faces they see are the angels assigned to transport them to the next life (Luke 16:22). When Stephen, the deacon, was being stoned to death, seconds before his spirit departed, he looked up, and in a vision, he saw Jesus, "standing on the right side of God" (Acts 7:55). As the final stone struck his head, leaving him unconscious unto death, the last face he saw in the vision was Jesus, and the first face he saw in paradise was Jesus! At death, the angels transport you, and the Lord welcomes you!

WILL GRAVES BURST OPEN?

There have been varied opinions as to what will occur the moment of the resurrection of the dead in Christ. When Christ rose from the dead, we read:

> "And the graves were opened; and many bodies of the saints which slept arose, and came out of the graves after his resurrection, and went into the holy city, and appeared unto many."
>
> – Matthew 27:52-53

The graves in Christ's time were not the same as our contemporary graves. Now, the departed are laid to rest several feet under the ground. Known as a sepulcher, individual tombs were carved inside of a limestone type cave, formed by cutting a long niche, large enough to place inside of it a body that was wrapped in linen. Often, one catacomb was prepared for an entire family. Notice that "many" of the saints arose, and not "all" of the saints in Jerusalem. *These saints were individuals who had died within a short period of time before or near the time of Christ's death.* This does not appear to be a resurrection where their bodies had turned to dust and were reformed as they "appeared unto many," alluding to appearing to the living who had personally known them.

Christ's resurrection preceded these saints yet occurred at the same time. Christ is called the "firstfruits of them that slept" (1 Cor. 15:20). Firstfruits is the third festival of Israel. It celebrates the first ripened barley that is harvested and presented by the High Priest to the Lord at the temple. Gathering the first of the harvest for the Lord caused the remaining field of grain to be set aside as blessed.

These first saints to be raised with Christ that died under the old covenant (or the old order before the crucifixion) where the righteous souls concealed under the earth. Matthew said many "bodies of the saints" arose. These were the same bodies that had been wrapped in linen and laid in the limestone catacombs in Jerusalem. These individuals, although unnamed in Scripture, were known by other saints living in Jerusalem.

Whatever happened to these individuals? There are three schools of thought. The first theory is that they were with Christ when He preached to the spirits confined under the earth, and when He arose, they arose with Him, later being presented to God in heaven as the firstfruits. Them being taken to heaven could have occurred at the conclusion of Christ's forty days when He ascended to heaven (Acts 1:3-9).

The second theory is that they were seen for a brief time and ascended when Christ informed Mary that He was ascending to the Father, which He did between the time He spoke to Mary, and the time

He met with Thomas (John 20:17). We are uncertain as to how long Christ was with the Father in heaven before returning to earth, as this was the time when He sprinkled His blood on the sacred furniture in heaven, preparing access for those who would believe in Him (Heb. 9:12). If this was the timing, then Christ presented these saints as His "firstfruits" (of the resurrection) at the temple in heaven, around the *actual time* of the festival of firstfruits!

The third theory says that these saints were raised as Lazarus was. A select group had been dead a few days, and their *physical bodies were still intact* and were not yet in a complete state of corruption. When Christ arose, He brought the soul and spirit of a limited group of the dead out of Abraham's bosom (Luke 16:22), enabling them to walk the streets as a testimony of Christ's resurrection power. If these individuals were raised similar to Lazarus, then they would have passed away again (as Lazarus did), where at death, their spirits would be taken to the heavenly paradise located in the upper heavens and not confined in a chamber under the earth.

The law of firstfruits is significant. Paul refers to Christ being raised from the dead and calls Christ the "firstfruits of them that slept" (1 Cor. 15:20). When a "firstfruits" was offered on the temple altar, a spiritual principle was released. The entire field was not yet harvested. Only a small portion of what was ripe had been taken. However, obedience to the law of firstfruits released a supernatural blessing on the remaining part of the field later to be harvested. The remaining field would be blessed because the first was presented to God at the temple. Christ bringing forth the firstfruits of His resurrection sanctified all of the others who would die in Him. Every cemetery holding the bodies of the righteous would one day hear Christ's voice, and they would be raised!

At the resurrection, a person will have a new body that will be exempt from the corruptible pain, suffering, sicknesses, and other despairing manifestations.

CHAPTER FIVE

WILL YOU BE NAKED OR CLOTHED AFTER DEATH?

This may come as a strange question, and perhaps you have never considered this before. When a person dies, their body is usually clothed. If they pass away at work, they may be wearing their uniform. If their departure was from home, they could be wearing casual clothes. If their last moments were spent in a hospital or a special care facility, they might be clothed in a hospital gown. Obviously, at death, no one takes their clothes with them, which leads to the question, are the soul and spirit completely uncovered, or naked when it departs, or is there some form of a covering the human spirit receives once separated from the body?

There is a case that some make for the "naked spirit theory." In Eden, when God created Adam and Eve, Moses wrote that they were both "naked and not ashamed" (Gen. 2:25). The first thing they both noticed after eating from the forbidden tree of knowledge of good and evil was that they were both *naked* and immediately sewed fig leaves together, forming aprons covering their bodies (Gen. 3:7). Later, when God confronted Adam, who was concealing both himself and Eve among the trees, he confessed that he "knew he was naked" and was hiding from the Lord (Gen 3:10). Most believers pay little attention to the conversation before Adam and Eve were expelled, especially about the issue of them being naked before and after the fall. God even asked in Genesis 3:11, "Who told you that you were naked? Have you eaten of the tree that I told you not to eat from?"

Some theologians suggest that although both were naked, they were "covered" with a covering of the glory of the Lord, which was some form of light. When sin came, this "glory covering" was removed, and they saw themselves in a manner they had never seen before. This, of course, is speculation and cannot be proven in Scripture. It is clear, however, that God slew two animals and covered the nakedness of Adam and Eve, and from that moment on, clothing was worn.

When an infant is born into the world, it is born without clothing as this is provided by the parent or guardians. At death, there is no clothing transfer, only an outfit worn at the funeral. However, there are special garments worn in heaven, as indicated when John saw the martyrs who were slain on the earth:

> "When He opened the fifth seal, I saw under the altar the souls of those who had been slain for the word of God and for the testimony which they held. And they cried with a loud voice, saying, "How long, O Lord, holy and true, until You judge and avenge our blood on those who dwell on the earth?" Then a white robe was given to each of them; and it was said to them that they should rest a little while longer..."
>
> – Revelation 6:9-11 (NKJV)

These individuals gave their life on earth by being beheaded for their faith (Rev. 20:4). At death, their souls were taken to heaven and were placed in a specific location, which John revealed was located under the crystal floor and under the altar of God. Notice they are all given a "white robe" to wear and were told to "rest" for a season. This indicates that the white robes are given *once the person enters the heavenly paradise.*

Throughout the book of Revelation, John observed that there were individuals from the earth that were worshipping in heaven, and in each case noted, they were all in white robes or white garments (see Rev. 7:9; 19:8). In one of the messages to the seven churches, John was informed that if a person would "overcome," they would be "clothed in white raiment..." (Rev. 3:5). There is a reason for the color white being used. At the future heavenly marriage supper, all attendees will be clothed in "fine linen, clean and white: for the fine linen is the righteousness of saints" (Rev. 19:8). According to Daniel, God Himself is clothed in a white garment that is white as snow (Dan. 7:9). Christ will return to earth at the conclusion of the tribulation riding a "white horse." This concept was not new, as during the Greek-Roman culture, certain emperors or military generals conquering another army or seizing a nation, would enter the city riding on a white stallion.

When visiting the garden tomb in Israel, the traditional site of Christ's tomb, I speak on the resurrection of Christ and remind the visitors that Christ's body was wound in linen and He was placed on the stone slab inside the tomb naked and wrapped in linens (John 19:40). However, when Mary saw Him shortly after His resurrection, she thought He was a gardener, indicating that Christ was dressed in a special set of garments that had been given to Him by someone after He arose and left the linen grave clothes on the stone slab. Where and when did Christ clothe Himself before seeing Mary?

Perhaps Scripture from the Torah will answer the question. Christ was the new High Priest that would sit in heaven, making intercession for us. In Exodus, the earthly High Priest was clothed in eight garments of beauty throughout the year, except on the Day of Atonement when he would remove his colorful garments replacing them with four, white linen garments, used for entering the Holy of Holies. These four garments were linen pants, a linen robe, a linen belt, and a headdress. I suggest this is the same type of garment Christ was wearing when Mary spotted Him next to the tomb, as He would soon ascend briefly back to the Father to sanctify the sacred heavenly furniture and would require these types of garments as the High Priest of our faith.

There were three angels, the first rolled the stone away (Matt. 28:2), and second and third were spotted inside the grave, one at the head, the other at the foot of the rock slab where Christ had laid. The only logical answer to where Christ's garments came from, is that they were provided by God Himself, given to the angels who handed them to Christ the moment He arose. Just as white robes are "given" to the martyrs upon their arrival in paradise, Christ was given these "priestly" garments the moment He was raised. There is yet another possibility as to the clothing received once the spirit exits the body.

Christ noted that a poor beggar died and was escorted to his eternal resting place by angels, meaning more than one (likely two). These angels engaging in the spirit-body-separation process could bring any type of garment with them to clothe a spirit once it exits the body. The idea of wearing a robe type garment is perhaps new to the more western-oriented mind. In western culture, jeans and a t-shirt are common. However, in many parts of the world, especially the Middle East, including the Gulf States, both men and women wear robe type garments. Arab men wear a thawb, which is a long tunic. The women in Muslim nations wear a black abaya, which is a loose-fitting, full-length robe. In both Testaments, men and women wore garments in the form of robes.

It is, however, possible that when a person arrives in heaven, they may dress according to the particular culture they are from. Several times throughout my life, the Lord has allowed me to experience very detailed dreams of heaven. Some were so specific that I actually thought I had died and was taken to the celestial world. In one instance, I saw an area where those who pass are taken to a special room where loved ones who knew them, meet them again — sort of a homecoming with family and friends. In this particular dream, I saw several women from the United States that had been killed during the 9-11 attacks. One unexpected observation was they were not all in white robes but were wearing the most colorful and expensive-looking dresses that I had ever seen. The colors were far brighter, and the fabrics seem to have a silk appearance. When I awoke, I thought, "If the Lord prepares this type of clothing for women in the west who pass away, they will all be extremely excited since most women I have met love shopping for new clothes!"

Since the book of Revelation speaks only of white robes and white garments, the assumption is that this is the only type of garment worn in heaven. Perhaps this is where Paul's words are important when he wrote that "eye has not seen, ear has not heard, neither has it entered into the heart of man the things which God has prepared for those who love him..." (1 Cor. 2:9).

Other verses emphasize the color white. Three times, the white garments are alluded to in the message to the seven churches (Rev. 3:4, 5, 18). Christ told the church at Sardis, for those who had not defiled their garments (righteousness), they would walk with Christ in white (Rev. 3:4), and the "overcomer shall be clothed in white raiment" (Rev. 3:5). The wearing of white robes, linen, and garments is mentioned eight times in Revelation. There is a strong emphasis on the garments worn being white.

The angel inside Christ's tomb was wearing a "long white garment" (Mark 16:5). At the transfiguration, the garment of Christ was "white and glistening" (Luke 9:29). Matthew added that Christ's face was shining like the sun, and "His raiment was white as the light" (Matt. 17:2). Mark also added a statement about the transfiguration. He wrote, "His raiment became shining, exceeding white as snow; so that no fuller on earth can white them" (Mark 9:3). A fuller was responsible for cleaning, shrinking, or thickening new wool and also dying cloth. There was a special soap used that would help a fuller remove stains from a white cloth (Mal. 3:2).

The heavenly garments are shiny and brilliantly white. So white that they seem to radiate light. Why must white be the color of the heavenly garments? The simple answer is that pure white represents the "righteousness" of the saints (Rev. 19:8). Isaiah said, "Though your sins be as scarlet, they shall be white as snow..." (Isa. 1:18). The choice of white is interesting, as this color would show the slightest stain. I have worn white shirts with ties for years. Any type of liquid, except water, will show up on the shirt as a stain. In Revelation 3:4, spiritual garments can be "defiled." In Greek, the word defiled here means to soil with a dark spot.

Peter prayed that we would be found "...in peace, without spot, and blameless" (2 Pet. 3:14). The word *spot* here in Greek is *aspilos* and alludes to being *unblemished spiritually and morally*. The word spot is used by Paul in Ephesians, where he said Christ desired to present a church that was without "spot, wrinkle, or any such thing." This Greek word *spot* is *spilos* and refers to some type of blemish or defect that figuratively leads to *disgrace* or embarrassment. To avoid a spotted garment, you must confess and repent of your sins. In Revelation 7, a multitude came out of the Great Tribulation, and John said they had "washed their robes and made them white in the blood of the lamb" (Rev. 7:14). This word "washed" is the Greek word *pluno* and means "*to flow or to plunge*," and can refer to the launders cloth a fuller would use to remove stains! Some Greek scholars teach that these individuals missed the return of Christ, for the overcomers, as their garments (righteousness), were stained, and they cleaned their robes (their walk with God) through repentance and the washing of Christ's blood.

In heaven, the twenty-four elders are clothed in white (Rev. 4:4), those coming out of the Great Tribulation are wearing white (Rev. 7:9). The seven angels with the last seven plagues are clothed in white linen (Rev. 15:6), and the saints at the marriage supper of the Lamb are all wearing linen garments that are "clean and white" (Rev. 19:8).

Sin creates a stain in the spirit that must be removed through repentance and confessing the blood of Christ. Repentance and confession will cleanse you from unrighteousness. Being presented with a white robe in heaven indicates that you have been made clean and worthy to enter the heavenly kingdom by receiving the forgiving power of the blood of Christ.

CHAPTER SIX

DID GOD KNOW YOU BEFORE CREATION?

What is the human spirit, and how or when did it originate? Let's go back to the beginning of human time. God
"formed man from the dust of the earth," meaning He
molded Adam's body into a form that was similar to Himself. God has
eyes that see, a mouth that speaks, hands, feet, and features that were
like those formed on Adam's body. This verse indicates the fact that
"man was made in God's image and God's likeness" (Gen. 1:26-27). The
Hebrew word *image* means "a resemblance, a figure of, and a represen-
tation." It is also used in the Old Testament in reference to an idol that
is cut or molded from clay, formed into an image to represent a person
or an animal. The Genesis story explains that God made a likeness of
Himself, not an earthly god but a fleshly man, in His "likeness." The
word likeness here alludes to the *form or the shape*. In modern terms,
we would say He made a *replica* of Himself.

Adam's "form" laid lifeless on the ground until God preformed
one significant act. He "breathed into man's nostrils the breath of life;
and man became a living soul" (Gen. 2:7). The Hebrew word for *breath*
is *neshamah* and refers to wind, including divine inspiration, and is
translated as "soul" and "spirit" in various Old Testament verses. God
"breathing" was a single act, and His "breath" entering Adam created
an eternal being and not just a mortal man.

GOD'S BREATH IS ETERNAL

The *lifeforce* keeping the physical body alive is concealed in the blood (Lev. 17:11). The lifeforce providing a man an eternal spirit is God's breath, which becomes the eternal spirit within each person. If the human spirit was released from the body and could be seen by others, it would look like a duplicate of the person it resided in, with the exception of the layers of excess fat that covers the body (which is part of the physical man and not the spirit man). A simple example is when a child breathes air into a balloon, the limp rubber object has a form that cannot be discerned until the breath from the child fills the balloon. Once the balloon is filled, the full shape is seen. God first created Adam's form, then breathed the "breath of life," bringing awareness, reasoning, knowledge, and life to the clay form.

Adam would have lived on earth in his physical body forever had he not sinned, and if he had continued eating from the "tree of life" (Gen. 2:9). The word "life" in this phrase is the Hebrew word *chay* from a root word that means to live or to keep alive, to revive. The tree of life in heaven has twelve different types of fruit that grow each month (see Rev. 22:2, 14). When Adam sinned, God assigned an angel (Cherub) to guard the tree of life. God warned that Adam could "put forth his hand, and take also of the tree of life, and eat, and live forever" (see Gen. 3:22). Before sinning, the tree of life continually revived Adam, renewing his body, soul, and spirit. Adam lived to be 930 years of age (Gen. 5:5). Perhaps because of his time in the garden, the residue of supernatural-nourishment from the tree of life continued for a long season, renewing his body for hundreds of years. All of Adam's bloodline, for nine generations before the flood, lived extremely long lives, as a bit of the DNA of Eden was passed on from Adam to his earliest descendants.

On the sixth day of creation, Adam's soul and spirit were imputed into his body of clay. The moment God breathed His breath out, life entered Adam. Each living human has a flesh body with an eternal spirit and a living soul residing within them. One of the greatest mysteries, debated for centuries, is where did the human soul and spirit originate, and when does God insert these two eternal forces within a child inside the womb? Some suggest the human spirit enters the moment of conception, while others teach this lifeforce enters the fetus approximately six months in gestation. Others hold the view that the body is formed in the womb, and God brings the spirit the moment the infant breaths on its own outside of the womb.

It would require a book of substantial size to dissect each theory explaining numerous Hebrew and Greek word studies, Biblical narratives, and the different points of view. My Biblical research indicates the spirit and the soul enter at the moment of actual conception. Our subject, however, will center on the question, did our eternal spirit pre-exist at the beginning of time with God, to then be placed in the womb at the moment of conception?

GOD'S FOREKNOWLEDGE

Two significant, often debated Biblical words, are *predestination* and *foreknowledge*. Predestination is the belief that God has foreordained all that will happen in a person's life. Some ministers go as far as to teach that certain people are preordained to receive salvation, and others preordained never to be converted to Christ. They use various examples, including Paul. They say that although Paul was a Pharisee with great hatred toward Christians, God ordained him from his mother's womb to become an Apostle in the Christian faith (see Gal. 1:15). Thus, he was "predestined" to be saved. On the opposite end, Christ chose Judas as one of His twelve Apostles. Judas held the important ministry position of serving as the treasurer for Christ's traveling ministry team. Christ, however, identified Judas as a "devil" (John 6:70 – which meant an adversary), and Christ commented that it would have been better for Judas to have never been born than to betray Christ (Mk. 14:21). When Judas later committed suicide, Peter pointed out that he "went to his own place," meaning a place prepared for him in hell (Acts 1:25).

It is noted that the Antichrist and the False Prophet are both future men who have *a predestined assignment* causing destruction and chaos on earth during the tribulation. Neither will have an opportunity to repent, but in reality are, as some say, "predestined for hell." These are three rare examples, and if all people were predestined for either heaven or hell, there would be no necessity for Christ's death and crucifixion to bring a redemptive covenant to offer salvation to sinners, and no need to preach the Gospel commanding men to repent. However, Christ commanded all believers and ministers to "preach the gospel to every creature" (Mark 16:15-16). Just as Esau *willfully chose* to give up his birthright, all men have a choice to accept or reject the message to repent and be baptized. God's predestined will is for you to *choose His will* and not your own.

KNOWN IN HEAVEN AND ON EARTH

Foreknowledge. This word refers to the ability to know something, such as facts, before the person or circumstance exists. In this case, we are talking about God's advanced knowledge about us before we were born. The Bible indicates that God knows each person long before they are formed in their mother's womb.

God informed the prophet Jeremiah, "Before I formed you in the womb, I knew you; before you were born, I sanctified you: I ordained you to be a prophet to the nations" (Jer. 1:5 NKJV). The word "sanctified" means to "set apart." Thus, before the prophet was formed in the womb, God set him apart for a specific task. The Hebrew word knew is *yada'* and refers to knowing in the sense of seeing something.

God "saw something" about Jeremiah before he was born. Was this foreknowledge simply God seeing (laying out) a plan, or did God see the spirit of Jeremiah in heaven before he was formed in a woman on earth?

One of the mysteries of "preexistence" is with Christ. Based on John 1:1-7, we understand the mystery that in the beginning, Christ was the "word" and existed with God from the beginning. Christ shocked the Pharisees when He said, "Before Abraham was, I am," and "Abraham rejoiced to see My day and saw it" (John 8:56, 58). God is a "spirit," and Christ, before He became flesh, was in heaven with God in the form of a spirit, not a fleshly body. How did the spirit of Christ, in heaven, end up coming to earth in the body of an infant? A verse in Hebrews explains this mystery:

> "Wherefore when he cometh into the world, he saith, Sacrifice and offering thou wouldest not, but a body hast thou prepared me."
>
> – Hebrews 10:5

The word *prepared* in this verse means "to frame, to join together." The Holy Spirit overshadowed Mary and placed the seed of God's Word in her womb. The body of Christ grew inside the womb of this blessed virgin for nine months. Christ, in some miraculous manner, was sent from heaven into the body of this infant! Christ was body, soul, and spirit and not just a physical body, as proven when He died, He "gave up" (released) His spirit (Matt. 27:50). At death, Christ's spirit departed His body and descended into the lower parts of the earth while His lifeless body was in the cold tomb (see Eph. 4:8-10). Christ was the "Word made flesh" (John 1:14). He was with God, came to earth, then returned back to God. In the beginning, while dwelling in heaven, He was God (a spirit). However, on earth, He was a man in a body, and following His resurrection, He was glorified in a resurrected body.

There is an interesting observation revealed by Solomon in Ecclesiastes 12:7. In the context of chapter twelve, Solomon is speaking about death. The key verse reads, "Then the dust shall return to the earth as it was: and the spirit will return to God who gave it." Solomon expresses that the spirit within the physical body was given (in the body) by God Himself. This means that the eternal spirit originated with God and His foreknowledge in *heaven*. When a righteous person dies, their spirit *returns* to God, and the body which is buried will eventually return to the dust (Gen. 3:19).

In Zechariah 12:1, the prophet spoke of God as the creator, saying that He stretched out the heavens and laid the foundation of the earth, and He "forms the spirit of man within him." God explained that He "formed" Jeremiah in the womb (Jer. 1:5), and here, Zechariah states that God also forms the spirit of a man within him. The idea concealed in the Hebrew word "formed" is that of clay on the potter's wheel. He takes the clay in his hands and begins forming a vessel that he visualizes in his mind. According to David, every part of your body was fashioned by the Lord, and all parts of each person are recorded in heavenly books:

> "Your eyes saw my substance, being yet unformed. And in Your book they all were written, The days fashioned for me, when as yet there were none of them."
>
> – PSALMS 139:16 (NKJV)

David spoke of "the book of the living" (Psa. 69:28), which is similar to the book where information of a person's future birth is recorded. The "substance" that forms the entire structure has been identified by scientists as DNA. However, who originated the DNA within the human cells that carry all genetic information? Only our creator could place such detailed information within the body.

David wrote a beautiful statement concerning his birth:

"For You formed my inward parts; You covered me in my mother's womb. I will praise You, for I am fearfully and wonderfully made; marvelous are Your works, and that my soul knows very well. My frame was not hidden from You, when I was made in secret, and skillfully wrought in the lowest parts of the earth.

— PSALMS 139:13-15 (NKJV)

These verses conceal numerous nuggets that attest to my subject. In this text, God was *forming* David of whom He has foreordained. God "covered" him from his mother's womb. The Hebrew word *covered* alludes to *setting a screen around something*, meaning God protected and "hedged him in" while his body was developing in his mother's womb. His "frame" here actually refers to his *conception* of which God was fully aware. The significant phrase is his *substance* (verse 16), meaning his unformed body. David reveals that God not only knew both his inward and outward parts, but they were also written in a heavenly book long before David existed on the earth. David knew that the number of days of his life were also set prior to the moment of his conception (Psa. 39:4). God's foreknowledge of you was set in the mind of God and in the books of heaven, even before creation!

To prove this, before Adam was created and the foundation of the world was laid, we read that Christ was the "Lamb slain from the foundation of the world" (Rev. 13:8), referring to the time God created the earth (Gen. 1:1). How is this possible? From Adam's day to Christ's birth, is about four thousand years. Another astonishing verse speaks of those whose names were "not written in the Book of Life from the foundation of the world" (Rev. 17:8). This raises the question, did God place names in the Book of Life long before the person ever repented? Peter explains it best when he wrote:

> "Forasmuch as ye know that ye were not redeemed with corruptible things, as silver and gold, from your vain conversation received by tradition from your fathers; But with the precious blood of Christ, as of a lamb without blemish and without spot: Who verily was foreordained before the foundation of the world, but was manifest in these last times..."
>
> — 1 PETER 1:18-20

Christ was slain 4,000 years after Adam. However, God's redemption plan was laid out before the creation of Adam. God, in His foreknowledge, knew what the first man (Adam) would choose, and God knew he would need redemption to obtain eternal life. Christ was foreordained before the world was created but was manifest as the sin solution about 4,000 years from the fall of man.

All of this deals with the foreknowledge of God. He is aware of us from eternity past, has plans for us during our lifetime, and desires that we spend eternity with Him.

All humans are formed in "the image and likeness of God." The first Adam is the earthly father of us all. Once we choose to follow Christ and repent of our sins, we are "born again of the Spirit" or, as Christ said, "born again" (John 3:3). The phrase "born again" is used three times (John 3:3, 7; 1 Peter 1:23). The Greek phrase used in John 3 is *gennao*, and it means to procreate, or figuratively to regenerate, which alludes to creating a new offspring. We become a "new creation" when receiving Christ (2 Cor. 5:17). We are created in God's image. However, when we receive Christ, we are "predestined" to be "conformed to the image of Christ" (Rom. 8:29).

Some believe that our eternal spirit preexisted with God. They believe that once it leaves heaven and enters an earthly body, a choice must be made as to where one will spend eternity, as this choice will ultimately reunite us eternally with God or seal the immortal spirit in eternal separation from God. An example would be the angels that fell (2 Pet. 2:4). All angels are spirits (Psa. 104:4), they ministered in heaven and were all present at creation (see Job 38:7). However, Satan initiated a major heavenly rebellion among the angels in which the rebellious angels were expelled forever to be separated from God. The Almighty had to prepare a place of confinement for these angelic spirit-rebels. The confinement is called hell. Jesus said that "hell was prepared for the devil and his angels" (Matt. 25:41).

Outside of the one reference of God breathing into Adam a "living soul," Jewish scholars note that there is not a direct reference to the origin of the soul or spirit; only implications alluded to that the eternal soul originates with God and is known by God prior to an infant being formed in the womb.

GOD'S BREATH IS ETERNAL

I have pointed out for many years that God is pure love, He is light, and He imparts eternal life. What comes forth *out of God* cannot die, as death is a result of sin, and death is God's enemy (1 Cor. 15:26). People often ask, "Why didn't God destroy Satan by simply annihilating him after he was cast out of heaven?" The answer is, angels are spirits, and a spirit-being is eternal and cannot be destroyed. They can only be separated from God. The Bible is the Word of God and came to us through Divine inspiration, as "all Scripture is given by inspiration of God…" (2 Tim 3:16). The Greek word "inspiration" comes from two Greek words, *Theos* (God) and *pneo* (breath out), meaning God breathed His breath out, causing the prophets and apostles to write under inspiration and revelation. This powerful lifeforce in God's spoken word, or in His breath, explains the verse, "Heaven and earth shall pass away, but my words shall not pass away" (Matt. 24:35). God's words can be fulfilled through His promises and prophecies, as His word came from within Him through His "breath." Prophecy in the Bible manifested when God breathed on the minds and spirits of the prophets. Since God's breath is tangible and has eternal characteristics, His spoken word continues to exist forever. Adam was a "living soul." Adam's body has long turned to dust, but his soul is still "living," to this day, in heaven's paradise.

God spoke the entire universe into existence. We read that He is "upholding all things by the word of His power" (Heb. 1:3). This is actually how the planets spin in the atmosphere, without falling apart, and remain on their course, as God is holding them up by His Word. This concept is in agreement with this verse, "by Him all things consist" (Col 1:17). This word *consists* refers to standing together or, as some suggest, *holding something together.* God's spoken word has the power to create something from nothing. Scientists who speak about the universe continuing to expand comes as no surprise to me. At creation, God spoke all things into existence, and God's command, "let there be light," is reverberating throughout the universe, still causing new stars to appear!

The human body is formed by a miraculous human process involving a tiny sperm and an egg. The body is physical and earthly in nature. The spirit and soul, however, must originate and come from God. It is the part that will never die. It will either live in heaven until the new earth, or it will be with those who do not have a redemptive covenant with Christ and will eventually be confined to the Lake of Fire (Rev. 20:15).

SEEING HEAVEN IN A COMA

One man who experienced being in a coma and seeing heaven was Ronnie Posey. My sister, Diana, interviewed him years before Ronnie passed away. The book of Revelation informs us that when believers from every age of time arrive in heaven, after the catching away, the resurrection of the dead, and Bema judgment, we will all be given a "new name" (see Rev. 2:17).

According to Ronnie, who explained how his soul and spirit visited paradise while in a coma, this new name given to each person was the *original name* God assigned to us when we were formed in the womb. Although our parents named us, God himself gave us a name.

While this concept is controversial among theologians, the spirits of men and women that existed with God's foreknowledge, are sent to earth from God into the wombs of women (Jer. 1:5; Luke 1:15; 1:31; Gal. 1:15). At death, the eternal soul and spirit will return to God. He will judge the spirit worthy of heaven or condemn it to be separated from Him. God has no pleasure in the death of a sinner (Heb. 10:38), as when a sinner dies, their soul is forever separated from God.

A new belief has emerged. After the Great White Throne judgment, those who are cast into the Lake of Fire will be annihilated and will cease to exist. This theory is based upon the idea that God would not allow someone to suffer eternally, and through His mercy, He will allow a person to become nonexistent. In Revelation 20, we read that being cast into the Lake of Fire is the "second death." This is taken to mean that they died once physically and will die forever once they enter the Lake of Fire.

If "fire" could destroy the soul and spirit, then all unrighteous individuals would have already "died" when entering the fire of hell (Matt. 18:8-9). Matthew 18:8 called this fire, "everlasting fire." This is the same

Greek word (everlasting) used for the term "everlasting" life (John 3:16; 5:24; 6:40). The word everlasting alludes to *unending time.* Christ spoke of "eternal damnation" (Mark 3:29) for those who blasphemed the Holy Spirit. The fire in both hell and the future Lake of Fire is literal and not a metaphor. However, this fire is "tormenting" in nature but does not consume the individual. When Christ spoke of individuals in hell, He warned, it was a place "where their worm does not die" (Mark 9:44).

The Greek word here for worm is *scolex,* and it refers to the worm that feeds upon a dead body. It is used three times, all by Christ (Mark 9:44, 46, 48). In the natural realm, the physical body returns to dust, and worms feed off of the body until it returns to dust, and eventually, the "worm dies." Christ's statement reveals that in hell, the person *never ceases from existence*, as the worm never dies.

In ages past, we know that God breathed into Adam the "breath of life," and he instantly became a living soul. The human spirit is no doubt linked with the breath of God, and I believe conception is when the spirit enters the womb of the mother. It would require something mysterious for the sperm and the egg to produce life. This mystery must be the breath of the almighty. Job 34:14 brings out an interesting insight:

> "If he (God) set his heart upon man, if he gather unto himself his spirit and his breath."
>
> – Job 34:14

The Hebrew word breath here is translated in the KJV as both soul and spirit and alludes to God's divine breath. David wrote, "...you take away their breath, they die and return to dust" (Psalm 104:29). The word breath here is *ruwach,* which is translated as wind, breath, or spirit. In Hebrew, God's Holy Spirit is called the Ruwach. When God removes the human spirit from the body, death is initiated. The

Psalmist also penned, "His (man's) breath goes forth, he returns to the earth, in that very day his thoughts perish" (Psa. 146:4). God breathed in Adam's "nostrils," and he became a living soul (Gen. 2:7). Job may have alluded to this when he wrote, "All the while my breath is in me, and the Spirit of God is in my nostrils" (Job 27:3).

It is clear that God breaths His breath, causing life to be initiated within the body. If the human spirit was not literally in preexistence with the Almighty from the foundation of the world as some teach, then it is clear that each person was known in the foreknowledge of God from the foundation of the world.

CHAPTER SEVEN

CAN YOU KNOW THE DAY THAT YOU WILL DIE?

N ew discoveries are always being made. There are new types of blood testing connected with DNA studies that claim they can determine the age in which you will die based upon family history, personal lifestyle, and specific DNA markers. Other tests allegedly claim they can determine if there are certain genetic markers in your blood that reveal a future form of Cancer, Parkinson's, or Alzheimer's. How would your life change if you knew the actual year and day that you would die?

In Scripture, several noted men were aware of the *actual day* in which they were to face death, making their departure to the other world. Elijah was informed of both the day and the method in which he would depart. Strangely, even the sons of the prophets whom he taught in prophetic schools were knowledgeable of this event. The sons of the prophets living at Bethel and Jericho made the same statement to Elisha, a student of Elijah in 2 Kings 2:3-5 (NKJV) saying, "Do you not know that the Lord will take away your master from over you today?" Elisha, also being aware of Elijah's departure, determined he would follow Elijah across the Jordan River and was present the moment Elijah was transported to heaven in a chariot (2 Kings 2:6-8).

In Psalms 68:17, we read that the "chariots of God are twenty thousand, even thousands of angels: the Lord is among them." Elijah was transported to heaven in a chariot of fire pulled by spirit horses who were also called "horses of fire." Elisha watched this transition and cried out, "My father, my father, the chariot of Israel and the horsemen thereof" (2 Kings 2). Why was this particular chariot called, the chariot of Israel? The name Israel was the name given by an angel to Jacob the night he wrestled one, and the angel prevailed against him. Israel was actually Jacob's new name, and his twelve sons, who formed a new nation, began populating their own individual tribes and were called, "The children of Israel." The chariot of Israel could well be the chariot that was sent to collect the soul of each individual patriarch of Israel, from Jacob forward at the moment of their death.

In a rather bizarre narrative, King Saul sought out a witch possessed with a familiar spirit to conjure up Samuel, as the Holy Spirit had departed from Saul, and the Lord was not speaking in any form to the backslidden king. The witch's eyes were opened, and she described "gods" coming up from the earth (1 Sam. 28:13). While some suggest the spirit that came up from the underworld was Samuel, this spirit was not a departed person, but a "spirit" identified in Scripture as a "familiar spirit" (Lev. 19:31; 20:6; Deut. 18:11). This spirit had access to two realms: the above-ground level filled with human information, and the underworld, the habitation of some evil spirits, fallen angels, and the spirits of those who had died. Prior to Christ's crucifixion, the spirit of both the righteous and unrighteous dead were confined under the earth in two separate chambers (Luke 16).

The witch described this familiar spirit as an old man covered with a mantle (1 Sam. 28:14). Saul never actually saw this spirit, but he "perceived" (or thought) it was Samuel. This spirit knew that the Lord's presence had departed from Saul, that David would become Saul's replacement, and was also aware that Saul had lost the Lord's anointing by not obeying God's instruction to slay the evil tribe of Amalek (1 Sam. 15; 28:18). All of these were *past events* that were publicly known, including specific judgments from God pronounced against Saul when the prophet Samuel was still living. It was also Samuel who anointed David to become Saul's future replacement. This particular spirit also knew Saul's death was imminent when it revealed that the opposing army would slay Saul and his sons the following day (1 Sam. 28:19). Thus, the information revealed was already known, with the exception that Saul would die the following day.

Christ also understood that according to specific Messianic prophecies (Psa. 22 and Isa. 53), He would die. He knew the physical suffering, coupled with the mental anguish that would befall him. Based on the Biblical types and shadows revealing He was the "Lamb of God" (John 1:29), Christ understood that Passover would be the set time for His suffering. He also informed His disciples that He would be three days and nights in the heart of the earth, and then He would rise again (Matt. 16:21; 20:40; 26:61). The spiritual principle of two or three witnesses establishing a word is confirmed when God sent Moses and Elijah to Christ, where they discussed His death in Jerusalem (Luke 9:30-31).

DEATH WARNINGS AND PREMONITIONS

Some individuals may actually receive a premonition (an advance feeling that something is about to happen), indicating their life on earth is coming to a conclusion. At times, this revelation is set and unchangeable, and at other times, the date can be altered through prayer. For example, the prophet Isaiah came to King Hezekiah and warned him to "set his house in order" because he was going to die. The king was suffering from some terminal infection that had formed a dangerous sore on his body (perhaps cancer). Hezekiah, instead of accepting this word as his final fate, turned his face toward the wall in his palace, facing the direction of the temple in Jerusalem, and petitioned God to heal him. Before Isaiah could pass the middle court of the king's palace, God reversed the death sentence, sending Isaiah back to announce that the king had been given fifteen more years (2 Kings 20).

On several occasions, the Apostle Paul assumed that his departure (death) was near. He escaped a premature death from the hand of Aretas, the King in Damascus, who had prepared a garrison of soldiers to arrest him. The disciples lowered him off the wall late at night in a basket (Acts 9:24-25). A second escape was when the religious Jews from Antioch and Iconium drug Paul outside of the city, stoning him and leaving him for dead. The Lord's disciples began praying, and God supernaturally raised Paul from the dead. The following day he departed the area, journeying to a new ministry location (Acts 14:19-20). Much later, when Paul prepared to return to Jerusalem, the prophet Agabus, through the gift of the word of knowledge, warned Paul that he would be arrested and bound with his own belt upon arriving in Jerusalem. Paul's response was that he was not only ready to be bound but was also prepared to die for the Gospel (Acts 21:10-13). Paul knew the danger and prepared for the worst-case scenario, his martyrdom. Paul's set appointment to pass from this life had actually not yet come, even though his circumstances made it look like his death could transpire suddenly through a mob of angry religious zealots. Many years later, while in Rome, Paul wrote, "I am now ready to be offered, and the time of my departure is at hand" (2 Tim. 4:6), and he was beheaded.

There may be particular moments in our life when we become discouraged, despondent, physically sick, or emotionally strained. These moments plant seeds of despair that manifest into a loss of joy that deceives us into thinking our end is near. In Paul's case, he was arrested but not killed in Jerusalem. It would be years later, after being arrested in Rome, when he confessed that he had "finished his course," referring to running a race and crossing the finish line (2 Tim. 4:7). Even the prophet Elijah became so weary that he sat under a tree and requested that he would die (1 Kings 19:4).

In the early 1990s, I received a typed letter from my father telling me of a dream he had in which he was told that he had an injury in his heart. In the handwritten letter, Dad, who was not in any way a wealthy man (although he was rich in faith — James 2:5), left a request as to whom would receive his books, an old rifle, and a few other small items. The letter saddened me because it came across as a good-bye letter in which he was preparing for his death. Many years passed, and Dad did have heart surgery and lived an additional ten years. Dad felt his death was soon. Thankfully his lifespan was extended.

THE PATRIARCH'S MISSED THEIR TARGET DATE

In Genesis 25, Abraham was lying on his back, thinking he was about to transfer to another world. He had one final desire, to see his son Isaac get married. Abraham commissioned his servant to go on a journey to Syria to find a wife for his son, Isaac. The servant eventually returned with Isaac's beautiful bride. Oddly, Abraham recovered from his infirmity as we read where he remarried, fathering six sons through his new wife (Gen 25:1-4). Abraham's death came many years later when he expired at the age of 175 (Gen. 25:7).

Isaac had a similar "I'm going to die" experience when he grew old. In Genesis 27, Moses records that Isaac's eyes were dim, and he believed he would eat his last meal and die (Gen. 27:4). He requested Esau to prepare his favorite meal, and then he would close his eyes, and be gone. In the narrative, Jacob deceived his father and received Esau's blessing. Returning from the field, Esau realized his brother's deception and planned a retaliation to kill Jacob. The death threat sent

Jacob into exile in Syria. Twenty years later, when Jacob returned to the Promised Land with his two wives, his children, and a massive flock of animals, his father, Isaac, was still alive. Perhaps he was waiting all those years to see if Jacob would return (Gen. 27; 35:27). Isaac was 160 when he believed he was departing this life and died at 180. The blessed patriarch was given an additional twenty years!

When Jacob's favorite son Joseph was sold into slavery by his brothers, Jacob was told a lie that Joseph had been devoured by some wild animal. Jacob was so grieved that he warned his sons that he would "go down to the grave mourning for Joseph" (Gen. 37:35). Years later, the sons of Jacob were asked by Joseph to bring Benjamin to Egypt. Jacob, once again, entered a grieving state as observed in this statement, "If mischief befalls him (Benjamin) by the way in which you go, then you shall bring my gray hairs down to the grave" (Gen. 42:38). Three times Jacob spoke of his "gray hairs" and "going down to the grave" (Gen 42:38; 44:29; 44:31). For over twenty years, Jacob believed the lie that his favorite son was dead. When he discovered Joseph was alive in Egypt, his spirit "revived" (see Gen. 45:27). Jacob predicted that he would journey to Egypt, see his son, and then die. Jacob took the long journey, where he not only saw Joseph was alive, but he also met two of his grandsons who were born through Joseph that Jacob did not know existed. Instead of dying, his life was extended seventeen more years, and then he died in Egypt at the age of 147.

In each instance, there was a reason that these three patriarchs of faith incorrectly believed their death was imminent. For Abraham, his beloved wife passed. He felt lost without the love of his life (Gen. 23:19). Isaac's eyes were dim (actually he was going blind), and his health was deteriorating (Gen. 27:1). Jacob loved Joseph more than all of his other sons, as Joseph was the son of his beloved wife, Rachel, and the son of his old age. Believing Joseph had been killed brought mental anguish and emotional pain. This senior man was grieving himself to the point of death. Emotions of sadness and grief zap the joy and vision from us.

Often, when we encounter a negative family experience, a sudden tragedy, the premature death of a close friend, or a loved one, it feels like a section of our heart has been removed from us, creating a strange void, an emptiness. We become washed over with discouragement and mixed emotions resulting in depression and oppression. A spirit of hopelessness and despair can deceive us into thinking that our own demise is near, and the angel of death has our address in his Rolodex. Just because you have a sense or a premonition of death, does not guarantee you have an advanced warning of your departure. You should live to fulfill your assignment and never accept an early departure when you have not completed the will of God.

REVERSING A DEATH SENTENCE

We know it is "appointed unto men once to die" (Heb. 9:27). The English translation of the Bible uses the word *appointed* in *twenty-three verses*. There are numerous Greek words used in the New Testament that translate to "appointed" in English. The Greek word used in Hebrews 9:27 is different than the other words. It refers to something that is *reserved in the future that you are waiting for*. It is something *laid up in store* for a person. A death appointment is a specific time set by a divine decree.

Only two men have escaped death: the first being the seventh descendant from Adam, Enoch. At age 365, God translated him to heaven. Enoch's translation is referred to in Genesis 5:23-24 and Hebrews 11:5. The second prophet, Elijah, was transported to the celestial world in a supernatural chariot of fire drawn by spirit horses (2 Kings 2:11). Both men escaped death. Most Evangelical prophetic scholars believe these two men will return to earth during the first half of the Great Tribulation, identified as the two witnesses alluded to in Revelation 11:1-2. Both will be slain by the Antichrist at the end of their forty-two-month ministry.

When it comes to one's appointment with death, there are three possibilities:

1. Dying prematurely before the appointed time

2. Dying at the appointed time

3. Extending life at death beyond the appointed time

Solomon asked the question, "Why should you die before the time?" in Eccl. 7:17. This wise man warned of being "overly wicked," and "foolish," implying that wickedness and foolishness are a slippery slope that can drag you into premature death.

Many celebrities, musicians, and "stars" party themselves into an early grave by experimenting with drugs or drowning their boredom with bottles of alcohol, shortening their lives by destroying their bodies. It is quite possible to die before your time. When my loved one was in the emergency room for a very unwise decision he made, the doctor, who attended my home church in Cleveland, informed me that eighteen teenagers from Bradley County and surrounding counties in Georgia, had taken the same type of pills he had and they never made it out of the emergency room alive.

We read where Abraham "died in a good old age" (Gen. 25:8). Gideon also "died in a good old age" (Judges 8:32). When King David passed from this life, we read, "And he died in a good old age, full of days, riches and honor..." (1 Chron. 29:28). A person who has a redemptive covenant through Christ is given the promise of a long life. One of the Ten Commandments reads, "Honor your father and mother that your days may be long upon the earth" (Exod. 20:12 NKJV). Those who abide in the Lord are told, "With long life will I satisfy him and show him my salvation" (Psa. 91:16 NKJV). By obeying and living out the instructions commanded in the Word of God, we are given a promise in Proverbs 3:1-2, "Length of days and long life, and peace, shall they add to you." There is a *set time* to die, and that time should arrive *after* we have lived a long life. In Psalms 90:10, we read that "man's days are seventy and by reason of strength eighty." My father noted that this was not written to set a limitation on how long one would live, as there is no set limitation, and life can be extended "according to one's strength" (Psa. 90:10).

Our life can be extended by making good choices, breaking unhealthy habits, and taking special care of our body, mind, and spirit. I recall an incident related to a great man of God, Steve Hill, the Evangelist during the great Brownsville Revival (1995–2000). Steve was diagnosed with cancer, and after much prayer, began receiving treatments. I remember him calling me and telling me that he was given a short time to live but had asked God to extend his time so he could win more souls. Despite his physical infirmity, Steve received strength to continue for many months, winning the lost and writing his final book, Avalanche.

One of my former office workers, Iris, was a great woman of God. Many years ago, in 1965, when she was 38, her father Bill Lawson was in the final stages of cancer, dying in an Albany Georgia hospital. He had become unconscious, and gangrene was setting into his body. Tumors the size of a cantaloupe and cancerous masses within his body were eating away at him. With his life slipping away, a group of strong prayer warriors, including Dr. T.L. Lowery, a noted revivalist, gifted in praying for the sick, came to the hospital room to pray for Bill. As Lowery stood beside the bed of this dying man, he prayed intently and suddenly gave a prophetic word:

"The storm is still raging. The lightning is still flashing, the thunder is rolling but fear not, for I am master of the ship. Remain in the ship, and I will raise you up as a testimony of my power, to this town and this community. I will place you on another plain where you will know and understand the reason for all of this."

Eventually, cancer gained its foothold, and Bill entered into a coma with only hours to live. His body suddenly began sweating water to the point that the hospital had to change his gown nine times in a few hours. When the darkest hour arrived, his eyes suddenly opened, and as if by supernatural help, he sat up in the bed saying, "Devil, get out of my back yard, I am not giving you an inch!" He lay back down as his body began quivering. His color began changing. Green bile began appearing on his gown. After a series of examinations, the doctors found no trace of any cancer or growths! Within five weeks, he gained fifty pounds and lived a long life. His wife held on to every promise of healing, praying, and believing without wavering.

Often when a loved one is facing a horrible disease, we don't ask for more time because we accept the bad report or are *uncertain of God's will* for the individual. Other family members are fearful of *being disappointed* and not seeing the requested results, and avoid seeking healing.

I believe we should fight the fight of faith for every year, month, hour, minute, and second that we can continue living and spiritually impacting others. When our moment arrives, may we say what Paul said, "I have fought a good fight, I have finished my course, and I have kept the faith" (2 Tim. 4:7). The biggest question you must ask yourself is, where will I end up for eternity? There are only two locations, and your choice will be determined in this life.

CHAPTER EIGHT

THE ROAD LEADING OUT: AMAZING WORD STUDIES CONCERNING DEATH

We all plan to remain alive on earth as long as possible. However, when the time arrives, we will leave here swiftly. There are two roads *leading out* from this life to the next; one is very narrow and straight, and the other is wide (Matt. 7:13-14). Your exit strategy must be prepared in advance, and the road you choose will determine either your ascent or descent when the road ends.

In 2 Peter 1:11 (NKJV), the Apostle Peter penned an interesting statement:

> "For so an entrance will be supplied to you abundantly into the everlasting kingdom of our Lord and Savior Jesus Christ."

The word *entrance* in the Greek means *"into the road,"* alluding to the road leading to eternal life with Christ in His eternal kingdom. There is a specific path required to lead a person on their journey into this heavenly kingdom. Christ called this a "straight gate and narrow way," it is a "path of righteousness" (Matt. 7:14; Psa. 23:3). The word *narrow* in Greek is *thlibo* and is sometimes translated in the KJV as "afflict, have trouble, or suffer tribulation." These words allude to being under some type of pressure, not just an inconvenience but a real hardship. The pressure on a righteous person to compromise does not come from God but is a satanic pressure to conform to the world, give in to carnal desires, including yielding to the temptations of the evil one. The adversary's goal is to pull you off the straight path. The narrow road that a godly person must walk on is narrow, not because there is no room for walking on it, but because a person must balance themselves in truth and righteousness to prevent being pulled aside to the left or right by the *pressure* to do wrong or give up.

In Peter's second epistle, he knew he was going to die, and his soul and spirit would exit his body. Paul also alluded to his death when he wrote in his final epistle, "My departure is at hand" (2 Tim. 4:6). The Greek word here for *departure* is *analisis*, and means *"to loosen, to undo, and break up."* In Paul's time, this Greek word was used as a military term when an army changed its location and moved a soldier's tent from one place to another. It could also be used as a nautical term, meaning "to lift anchor and loose the ship to another location."

Paul states that this departure from one location (earth) to another (the heavenly paradise) was "at hand." In western thought, this means "soon." However, the Greek phrase has a different nuance and means *"to stand and be on hand."* Paul was saying that death was standing nearby and would soon take him from one place to a new location. Soon after he penned these words, Emperor Nero beheaded him in Rome.

A NEW TABERNACLE

Now we read another revelation that the Apostle Peter penned in 2 Peter 1:13-14. He wrote:

"Yea, I think it meet, as long as I am in this tabernacle, to stir
you up by putting you in remembrance; knowing that shortly I
must put off this my tabernacle, even as our Lord Jesus Christ
hath showed me.

The Greek word Peter used for *tabernacle* is *skenoma, and it* refers
to a *tent.* Paul used this same word when describing his physical body
in 2 Corinthians 5:1 (NKJV):

"For we know that if our earthly house, this tent, is destroyed,
we have a building from God, a house not made with hands,
eternal in the heavens."

Peter, James, and John were present at the amazing transformation
of Christ. High on a mountain, Moses and Elijah appeared conversing
with Christ concerning the mystery of His death in Jerusalem. Matthew
writes that Jesus was "transfigured." The word used here is *"metamor-
phoo,"* which actually alludes, in this case, to Christ changing from one
form to another. These three eyewitnesses reported, when this meta-
morphosis occurred that Christ's face shone as "bright as the sun" and
His "garment began shining with light" (Matt. 17:1-2). Matthew reports
that, at the same time, a bright cloud (scholars note this cloud was similar to the cloud of God's glory), appeared in the tabernacle of Moses
and overshadowed everyone on the scene. From within this cloud, the
voice of God was heard speaking and revealing to all that were present
that Christ was God's beloved son (Matt. 17:5).

The transfiguration is often interpreted as a preview of the future
resurrection of the dead at the return of Christ. Moses had died, and
God buried him in the plains of Moab about 1,500 years prior to this
narrative (Deut. 5:5-7). Elijah, on the other hand, was supernaturally
transported into the third heaven in a chariot of fire (2 Kings 2). Moses
represents those who have died and will be resurrected from the dead.
Elijah's transportation to heaven represents that the believers who will

be alive will be "changed" in a moment, in the twinkling of an eye, at Christ's return (see 1 Thess. 4:16-17).

At the transfiguration, it was Peter who said, "Let us build three tabernacles." The Greek word *skene* is used for *tabernacles*. Why is "tabernacle" used to allude to a body? To answer this, we turn to the Old Testament, where Moses was instructed to build God a tabernacle using wooden boards and the skins of various animals as a covering.

When Moses' tabernacle was put up, it involved a three-fold process. First, the wooden posts were set in place. Then, the beautiful dyed animal skins of various colors were laid and hung, forming the curtains. Lastly, the sacred furniture was positioned in its proper location. This tabernacle is also a picture of the human body. The posts represent the bone structure of the body, the skins are the outer layer of skin covering our bones, and the sacred furniture is the internal soul and spirit that dwells within the body.

When the tabernacle was taken down to be reset in another location, the process was reversed from the setup. First, the sacred furniture was removed, then the skins were rolled up, and finally, the beams were pulled apart at their joints, making them easier to carry. This transferring of the tabernacle is a beautiful imagery of the departing of a believer!

First, the moment a believer passes from this life, the angels of the Lord separate their soul and spirit from their physical body (their earthly tabernacle). Eventually, the skin on the body turns to dust, and the last aspect of death is when the person's bones return to the earth. Just as a man-made tent does not last forever, the physical body of every living person will not last forever in this physical, earthly realm. Only at the resurrection does this mortal body of corruption become incorruptible as a new resurrected body.

THE FINAL EXODUS

Peter continued contemplating his death when he wrote these words, in 2 Peter 1:15:

"Moreover I will endeavor that ye may be able after my decease to have these things always in remembrance."

Peter used the word "*decease*." In English, it refers to a person who has died. The Greek word decease is *exodos,* and it means "the road out." It refers to an exit route. The Greek word translated as decease is also used In Luke 9:31, where Moses and Elijah are conversing with Christ, speaking to Him of His death, which would transpire in Jerusalem. We are told in Hebrews 9:27 that it is "appointed unto men once to die, but after this the judgment." The word "appointed" is used 23 times in the English translation. The Greek word used here is different than all the other times it is found, and it refers to a time that is reserved and laid up like an appointment.

It is interesting to note the word referring to exit or departing is very similar to the word we use to describe Israel's departure from Egypt. An entire book, the book of Exodus, deals with this departure and the events surrounding Moses receiving the law of God and instructions for the tabernacle as they journeyed to the Promised Land. The Exodus narrative covers an amazing revelation. Among the Hebrews in Egypt, the blood of a lamb applied on the outside doorposts of their homes protected the firstborn sons from the death angel. The following morning, they began a journey from the land of bondage to the land of freedom. Our "exodus" will be when our soul and spirit *depart* this earthly land of sin and sickness, being released from our body to make our journey to heaven, where our soul and spirit will await the resurrection of the dead!

WHY PEOPLE FEAR THEIR FINAL EXODUS

There is a silent fear that brews in the minds of many men and women when speaking about their departure from this life. There are numerous reasons, including the unknown factor as to what (if anything) lies beyond this life. It is interesting that many individuals will delay repenting, or even thinking about their eternal destination, until their death beds.

The Apostle Paul introduced us to the term "sting" of death. He wrote, "Oh death, where is thy sting? O grave, where is thy victory?" (1 Cor. 15:55). This word "sting" refers to pricking something at a certain point and is also figuratively used for what was called a goad; a long wooden club with nails on the end used to prod an animal when they refused to plow a field or carry a load. When Paul was arresting and resisting Christians, Christ appeared to him and said, "it is hard for you to kick against the pricks" (Acts 9:5). The word *pricks* in Acts 9:5 is the same word translated as *"sting"* in 1 Corinthians 15:55.

For a true child of God, death has lost its fear, and its sting has been removed. Each person must prepare their exit strategy. For a practicing sinner, one should never deceive themselves into thinking they have forever to prepare for the one appointment that they must face, an appointment with the angel of death. It is better to choose the straight path, and with the help of the Holy Spirit, walk therein, and in the end, make a successful exit from this life to the next.

ARE THE DEAD ACTUALLY DEAD?

Attending the funeral of a strong, dedicated Christian can be an interesting and moving event. However, as a child, my first funeral at Dad's church puzzled me. The church members were standing near the corpse resting in the coffin announcing, "He is not here he is with the Lord." I looked over in the box and thought, "Am I missing something here? They are in the coffin and not with the Lord. If they were with the Lord, the wooden chest would be empty."

It would be years later, after much research, that I understood their comments. The soul and spirit, at death, are absent from the body and present with the Lord. This is what Paul alluded to when he wrote of being "absent from the body" (2 Cor. 5:6-8).

ABSENT FROM THE BODY

Paul said he was willing to be "absent from the body and to be present with the Lord" (2 Cor. 5:8). In the 1611 English translation of the New Testament, the word "absent" is used in Paul's epistles ten times in ten verses. In seven verses, the word *absent* is the Greek word *apeimi*, meaning "to be away." In most verses, the word alludes to being physically away from a church or a group of people (1 Cor. 5:3; 2 Cor. 10:1). However, the Greek word in 2 Corinthians 5:6-8 (NKJV) is different with a different meaning:

> "So we are always confident, knowing that while we are at home in the body we are absent from the Lord. For we walk by faith, not by sight. We are confident, yes, well pleased rather to be absent from the body and to be present with the Lord."

In this passage, the Greek word *absent* is *ekdemeo*, and it refers to emigrating. The word indicates a transfer from one location to another. The Scripture teaches that our eternal citizenship is registered in the Lamb's Book of Life in heaven (Rev. 21:27). When departing from this life, our eternal soul and spirit must emigrate from the earthly world to the heavenly realm.

When Paul spoke of being "present" with the Lord, he used a Greek word that means "to be in one's own country, or to be at home."

Another way of rephrasing Paul's statement is "to be absent from my body is to be at home with the Lord."

At death, a person's body remains buried in the ground, and as time passes, it returns to dust, just as God told the first man Adam it would (Gen. 3:19). However, the soul and spirit migrate to an eternal home in heaven and will, at the resurrection during the return of Christ, rejoin with the DNA particles forming a perfected resurrected body.

Paul often found himself in a quandary. On the one hand, he understood the significance of his ministry among the Gentiles, which required him to remain on earth, preaching, instructing, and starting churches. At other times, he desired to be removed from his earthly body to be with the Lord in the heavenly realm. Part of this dichotomy of opinions might be a result of his heavenly visitation in which he had seen (either in a vision or an out of the body experience) the third heaven, into paradise, the location of righteous souls who have died. Paul saw amazing things, so intimate and unique that he was not permitted to reveal the details to people (see 2 Cor. 12:1-6).

Paul's occupation was a tentmaker (Acts 18:3). The sons of Jewish parents always learned a trade or profession while growing up. In Philippians 1:23-24 (NKJV), Paul reveals his struggle when he writes:

> "For I am hard-pressed between the two, having a desire to depart and be with Christ, which is far better. Nevertheless, to remain in the flesh is more needful for you."

He "desired" to be with the Lord, yet understands it is more beneficial to remain on earth for the believer's sake. The word Paul used for "*depart*" in the Greek means, "to take down one's tent and be off." Tents were used in both testament eras and are still used today, especially among nomads living in the deserts in the Middle East. The early patriarchs, Abraham, Isaac, and Jacob, all dwelt in tents. The entire tabernacle constructed by Moses was a portable tent that could be set up or packed up for traveling. Tents speak of a pilgrim journey as this term is used in Hebrews 11:13, where the writer lists the men of God who confessed they were "pilgrims and strangers on earth."

As people in covenant with God, we are the "strangers" on earth as our real home is in the third heaven where God Himself dwells. When Christ appeared on earth, John called Him, "The Word that became flesh and dwelt among us" (John 1:14). Greek scholars note that the word for "dwelt" in John 1:14 is not the usual Greek word meaning "to abide," but it comes from a verb meaning "tent." Some translate it as "the word was made flesh and tabernacled among us." This theme that the human body is a tent that houses the spirit is a theme found among numerous Biblical writers.

THE DEAD ARE ACTUALLY ALIVE

Because the soul and spirit dwelling within the bodies of men and women are eternal in nature, when a living person breathes their final breath of air on earth, their everlasting soul and spirit exits their body and enters into one of two dimensions. Scripture describes one of them as very foreboding, dark, evil, and wicked. The other is described as a realm of light, peace, and righteousness for those who are in covenant with God through Jesus Christ.

Often, when a person thinks of a Christian or the Christian faith, they see Christ as a man who organized a new religion, as Christianity is one of several major world religions. Those who do not understand Biblical doctrine, never comprehend the numerous reasons God sent Christ to earth. He did it to bring mankind a new redemptive covenant, to give the promise of eternal life to those who would believe in Him, and to prepare a place for us with the Father in heaven.

However, another important aspect of Christ and His message is to give hope to sinners, that through redemption, they would never be required to spend eternity in hell, separated from God.

Those who have passed are "alive" and are fully aware of the "other world" they are now in. The body was created to be in the earth and the soul and spirit for eternity. The body returns to the earth, but the righteous spirits return to God who gave them life (Eccl. 12:5-6).

CHAPTER NINE

THE MYSTERY OF THE HUMAN SOUL AND SPIRIT

A person has three distinct parts, all working together in one "body." 1 Thessalonians 5:23 (NKJV) tells us, "Now may the God of peace Himself sanctify you completely; and may your whole spirit, soul, and body be preserved blameless at the coming of our Lord Jesus Christ."

The writer of Hebrews speaks of "dividing the soul and spirit" (Heb. 4:12). For centuries, theologians have discussed the difference between the human soul and the spirit. Both the Old and New Testaments speak of the 'soul' and the 'spirit.' The first reference to the soul forming within a man was when God breathed into Adam, and he "became a living soul" (Gen. 2:7). The word "soul" is found 419 times in the English translation of the Old Testament, and all but one reference the Hebrew word "nephesh," which refers to a *living being*, both human and animals. Figuratively, it refers to the lifeforce that resides within a living creature.

The word Hebrew word 'spirit' is used and translated 244 times in our Old Testament English translation. The common Hebrew word is *'ruwach,'* which is translated as "wind, breath, and spirit." The meaning is determined by the context of how the word is used within the verse.

The Hebrew word spirit can allude to the spirit within a man (Dan. 2:1), the Spirit of God (Dan. 4:8), and the wind (Exod. 10:13).

In the New Testament, which was penned in the Koine (common) Greek Language, we see the words soul and spirit referenced. The word "soul" is mentioned in 36 verses and is the Greek word *psuche*, which also alludes to *breath* or the *lifeforce* that keeps a person or animal physically alive. It is connected with the heart, which in the Greek mind was the center for all life in the body. When the soul is sorrowful, it causes the heart to feel sorrowful. When the soul is joyful, the heart senses the joy. As believers, we are to love the Lord with all of our "heart, soul, mind, and strength" (Mark 12:30).

In the New Testament, the word *spirit* also holds numerous connotations. In 234 verses, the word can refer to the Holy Spirit (Matt. 4:1), the spirit of a man (Rom. 1:9), along with various forms of evil and unclean spirits (Luke 11:24), including the attitude expressed in a person (Luke 9:55). The word spirit is translated from the same Greek word, *pneuma*, which refers in most instances to a living spirit, such as God, angels, demons, and the human spirit. Jesus tells us that, "A spirit does not have flesh and bones" (Luke 24:39). Flesh and bones are the substance of a human body. However, the human spirit is housed within each human body. The proof that the spirit departs the body at death is evident at the crucifixion. Christ's last words were, "Father into your hands I commend (commit) my spirit" (Luke 23:46). At the moment of death, we read that Christ "gave up the ghost," meaning He released His spirit from His body (Mark 15:37). All four gospel writers record the events at the scene of Christ's crucifixion. Three reported that Christ "gave up the ghost" (Mark 15:39; Luke 23:46; John 19:30).

One of the first early church martyrs was Stephen. He was executed by stoning. Acts 7:59 tells us that as he was passing from the earthly to the heavenly realm, he was heard crying out, "Lord Jesus receive my spirit." Immediately, he requested that the Lord not lay the sin of his murder upon those who were responsible (Acts 7:60). The KJV says, "And when he said this, he fell asleep" (Acts 7:60). The words "sleep" or "asleep" are used in the New Testament as a metaphor for the death of the righteous. This was how the Jews described the death of a righteous person. This "sleep" was attributed to the body and not the soul or spirit, as the spirit of Stephen was received by Christ in heaven.

Moments before the separation of his spirit from his body, he saw a vision of heaven and said, "I see Jesus, standing on the right hand of God" (Acts 7:55). Christ is said to be "seated at the right hand of God" (Acts 2:34; Col. 3:1; Heb. 1:3; 10:12), indicating His redemptive work is finished and complete. Christ "standing" can indicate He is preparing to receive Stephen's eternal spirit into the heavenly paradise and is waiting for that moment when Stephen's spirit will be separated from his body. His spirit continues to live and has all five senses. He is aware, while his body appears to be "asleep," or sleeping the sleep of death.

SOUL AND SPIRIT — THE DIFFERENCE

The manner in which the words soul and spirit are used in the Bible make it difficult to distinguish the functional difference between the two. Paul, in the New Testament, refers to a spiritual man and a carnal man, which reveals the duel aspect of the human soul. The soul of a person tends toward an evil inclination and must be brought under the control of the spiritual inclination. This is the continuous struggle of carnality versus spirituality (1 Cor. 3:1-3). Either the earth will overtake heaven, and the carnal side will rule, or heaven will overtake earth, and the spiritual side will rule. One thing is certain. Death can't continue. One day, it will be the last enemy destroyed (1 Cor. 15:26), and life can't die, as eternal life means just that – eternal and unending. The body, however, is different.

The body without the spirit is dead (James 2:26). Since the separation of the soul and spirit from the body initiates a person's physical death, it is evident that the body borrows its lifeforce from the soul. The lifeforce maintaining the body is the blood, as the "life of the flesh is in the blood" (Lev. 17:11). The Hebrew word *life* in this verse is *nephesh*, which is the typical word translated as *soul* in the Old Testament.

Because memories are stored in the mind, or the soulish realm (not the body), this allows memories to continue to be recalled, even when the soul and spirit are outside of the body. This is clear in Luke 16. Abraham is conversing with a formerly rich man who died and was confined in the lower underworld compartment called hell. The man's body was buried on earth. However, his soul and spirit were very much alive in the world of departed spirits, in this chamber under the earth called Hades. The man could recall his former earthly life. He remembered that he had five living brothers on earth and wanted to warn them not to come to this place of doom (see Luke 16:19-31).

God is a spirit (John 4:24), angels are spirits (Heb. 1:7), and of course, demons are evil spirits. Spirits live in a dimension enabling them to take on various forms. In fact, the physical features of all humans originated with God, who created man in "His image and His likeness" (Gen. 1:26). Often, when a person thinks of a human spirit, they imagine it appears as some ghostly mist, a sort of fog in the shape of the person. The spirit residing within every person actually has a similar form and facial appearance of that person. Paul taught this in 1 Corinthians 13:12 when he stated that "face to face...I shall know, even as I am known."

It is interesting to note that on the Mountain of Transfiguration, three inner-circle disciples saw "Moses and Elijah." Moses had lived and died approximately 1,500 years prior to this event, and Elijah had been supernaturally transported to heaven around 800 years before appearing with Christ. The body of Moses was buried by God Himself (Deut. 34:5-6), and the physical body of Elijah remained in the same state it was when he was translated. Matthew indicates that when Moses and Elijah "appeared," they were both talking to Christ (17:3). Some scholars point out that Jesus called this a "vision," and the two prophets did not literally appear, but the disciples only saw an apparition. However, when the two prophets vanished, Jesus told Peter, James, and John to "tell no man the things you have seen" (Mark 9:9), meaning the three disciples literally saw these two prophets and were not hallucinating. Moments prior, the disciples were asleep and were suddenly awakened, "seeing" Christ's glory and the two men with Him (Luke 9:32). Moses would have been in a spirit form (as he had died), and Elijah still maintained a bodily form, as he was caught up to heaven alive in his body. To see any spirit form (such as Moses), the eyes of the individuals must be opened, and the veil of the invisible must be removed, as all spirits are invisible to the natural eyes.

When Christ appeared on the road to Emmaus speaking with two of His disciples, He suddenly vanished from their sight (Luke 24:31). This also occurred when Moses and Elijah suddenly vanished after speaking with Christ. Yet, to the Emmaus men, this was not a "vision" of Christ, but a literal appearance as was the appearance of Moses and Elijah. Luke also records where Christ appeared to Simon (Luke 24:34). The Greek word "appeared" is *optanomai*. The word can mean to "gaze upon something with open eyes," and carries the connotation of *gazing in amazement* and not just casually looking at something. There are other Greek words for appeared in the New Testament that mean to view something from afar and to observe something by looking at it.

I have always questioned how these three disciples knew the identity of these two men when the text makes no indication of who they were. They were "known as they were known," which confirms Paul's statement that when we stand face to face with Christ, our identity in heaven is linked with our identity on earth. Our heavenly rewards are presented to us at the Judgment Seat of Christ and are based on our works and deeds we performed while "in the body" (Rom. 8:13; 2:6). As people in covenant with Christ, our names are recorded in heaven in the Lamb's Book of Life. These "names" are our *earthly names*. Only after the judgment, do we receive a "new name" personally chosen by Christ for us (see Rev. 2:17).

Since we are all to be judged for our words, deeds, and actions, then it is evident that we carry with us, beyond this life and beyond the grave, the memories of our words, actions, and deeds, whether good or bad. When Christ reveals a word or action, we will be unable to say, "I don't recall that," the strategy used by some in a secular court case. It says, "the books will be opened," and we will be judged by what is "written in the books" (Rev. 20:12). Our actions and words become the evidence used, as it is written in Matthew 12:37, "By your words, you shall be justified, and by your words, you shall be condemned." Job said, "My witness is in heaven, and my record is on high" (Job 16:19). The word *record* here in Hebrew is *sahed*, and it refers to a *witness or means to testify*. We would say, "our testimony is in heaven." What we testify on earth is important, as the Bible says, we overcome Satan by the "blood of the Lamb and the word of our testimony" (Rev. 12:11). The Greek word *testimony* here refers to some type of confession that is used as judicial evidence. Satan is the accuser (prosecutor) before God day and night (Rev. 12:10). The blood of Christ, applied by our confession and repentance, removes the evidence of our guilt before God in heaven, rendering any charge against us useless!

SEEING OUTSIDE OF YOUR BODY

Medical doctors are often astounded when a patient who is pronounced *clinically dead* is revived. With their physical body considered dead and their heart not beating, some describe coming out of their physical body. They're either hovering above their body, watching the reactions of doctors, nurses, and surgeons, and some even describe seeing, in minute details, events and conversations that they should have no way of seeing or knowing.

One of the most dramatic, true cases involved a personal friend of mine named Richard Madison. Many years ago, he experienced a horrific accident. At the time, Richard was not a Christian, although his mother continually prayed for his salvation. Besides being mangled with broken bones and brain swelling, Richard was inactive, and in a coma. However, while in the coma, he could, at times, hear the conversations of people at his bedside, talking about his condition, unsure that he would "make it." He told me that one unforgettable incident was when a nurse was required to work on New Year's Eve. She was so upset. She came into his room and began cursing him because she had to care for him when she would rather be off work partying. He was in a coma, unable to respond, but heard what she said. After reviving, he told this nurse what she had said, much to her embarrassment.

Richard noted that while in the coma, at times, he would leave his body and walk the hallway of the hospital, hearing every conversation and seeing the activities near where he stood. On one occasion, he vividly recalled hearing his mother pray for his recovery and his salvation, and she was not in his room. His soul (or spirit) came out of his body and ended up in the small hospital chapel. He observed his mother kneeling and crying out to the Lord, asking God not to let her son die. He placed his hand on her shoulder, and she paused for a moment, turned, then continued praying. When Richard recovered, he told his mother of this incident. She immediately recalled praying in the chapel, wearing the same dress he described. She remarked, "At one point, I suddenly sensed a presence behind me, but turned and saw nothing."

Through the effectual and fervent prayers of many, Richard awoke from the coma, recovered from the accident, received Christ, and was led by the Lord into the ministry! Richard personally told me that through his experience, he knew that a soul and spirit resides in the body, and although a person might be in a coma, if their soul and spirit remain in the body, they can hear conversations. Family members should be cautious when speaking, as their loved one might hear what they are saying.

AN OUT-OF-BODY EXPERIENCE

The main Biblical reference as to how the human spirit can move and travel outside of the physical body comes from Paul. He revealed how he was "caught up into the third heaven," and was unsure if he was "in the body or out of the body" (2 Cor. 12:2-3). Out of the body alludes to his spirit coming out of his body and being transported to the third heaven for a brief period of time. In the body refers to his spirit remaining in his body, meaning he had a vision.

Paul relates that the episode of seeing paradise and the third heaven occurred about fourteen years prior to him writing his second epistle to the church of Corinth (2 Cor. 12:2). Scholars note that fourteen years prior, Paul was ministering in the city of Lystra, where he was stoned and left for dead (Acts 14:19). We cannot determine (neither could Paul) if he saw a vision of paradise the same way that John saw a vision of the Apocalypse, or if he temporarily died. If his experience was "out of the body," this means that he died from the stoning for a brief period, and his spirit was taken from his body to a special region in the third heaven called paradise, where righteous souls reside after their physical death on earth.

Paul's experience reveals that information from the earth is known in heaven, and information from heaven can be known on earth. In reality, this is how the Bible was written. Holy men of God, "spoke as they were moved by the Holy Spirit" (2 Pet. 1:21). The Apostle John was a prisoner on the Island of Patmos, surrounded by the waters of the Aegean Sea. He was suddenly "in the Spirit" and saw a vision of heaven where Christ was instructing him. He then heard the words, "Come up here" (Rev. 4:1-2) and was immediately caught up to the celestial world where he saw God's throne and numerous activities in the heavenly temple. John did not write his revelation in heaven but penned the Apocalypse from a cave on the Island of Patmos. However, this vision unfolded in the third heaven realm. How could his physical body be on an island located in the middle of the sea, yet a part of him captured not only the heavenly activity in the present tense (at the moment he saw it), but he stepped into a zone where the future, which would not occur for thousands of years, unfolded before him?

There is no indication that John was "out of his body," meaning his spirit had departed his body. He wrote, "After this, I saw…" (mentioned 35 times), meaning his spiritual eyes and understanding were opened to see clearly and to understand. The majority of these "out-of-body" experiences that we hear about involve the temporary death or near-death of a person. John's activities were linked with the ability of the soul and spirit to tap into a realm that is unseen by the eye, not heard by the ears, nor sensed by any normal bodily senses. The human eyes have a veil that prevents them from seeing into the invisible world of spirits. In reality, the spirit realm of God, angels, and demons is not "invisible." In the spirit dimension, they are quite visible as all spirits can see other spirits. God, who is a spirit (John 4:24), can see Satan, who is a fallen angel (Job 1-2). The Archangel Michael and his angels see and battle against Satan and his angels (Rev. 12:7-10). The only way a human can tap into visual sightings in the spirit world is if they experience a dream or a vision (such as we read in the book of Revelation), or if the "scales" that cover their human eyes, preventing them from seeing into the spirit world, are removed (such as the case of Elisha's servant – 2 Kings 6:17). Another possibility is when the soul and spirit are taken *outside of the body,* which is restricted by physical limitations. Once out of the body, the soul and spirit can then enter the higher level of the spirit world.

In most cases, the first time a redeemed believer will see an angelic being will be the moment of crossing over from physical death to eternal life. An example is when the poor beggar died at the rich man's gate in Luke 16, the angels separated his soul from his body, carrying the spirit of this beggar to Abraham's netherworld paradise. Exiting his body, this man saw both angels that were escorting him to his final resting place. God knew who he was, where he was, and when he died. He was ignored by a rich man but known in the domain of God and the angels.

At the moment of death, there will be several immediate visual sights every person will see. Since the human spirit consists of the same molecular structure as the angelic sphere, once outside of the body, the human spirit is empowered to clearly see into this once invisible world. The spirit dimension, or this invisible realm, is actually as real or more real than the material cosmos. In this other world, there is an entire galaxy and a heavenly civilization that exists. It has existed in eons past, even prior to the Luciferin rebellion that occurred at God's throne headquarters (Isa. 14:12).

The opposite realm is the netherworld. It was prepared in ages past under the crust of the earth and is the abode of spirits, fallen angels, lost souls, and demonic entities that are a part of this land of the lost.

Most sinners who have experienced a near-death or life-after-death encounter, speak of darkness, emptiness, fire, or a feeling of complete despair as they entered and viewed this other world that the Bible identifies as hell (Matt. 10:28; 18:9; Mark 9:43).

From years of research and from hearing numerous first-hand stories, here is what I believe to be the difference between the soul and spirit. The human spirit resides within the body. The *center* of the human spirit is in the belly area. We read, "The spirit of man is the candle of the Lord, searching all the inward parts of the belly" (Prov. 20:27). Christ spoke of the Holy Spirit dwelling within men and used this metaphor, "out of your belly shall flow rivers of living water" (John 7:38). The area of the belly is the center of the human spirit. Recently, researchers have discovered a "gut nerve" that connects from the area of the belly to the heart and the brain.

The human spirit is an exact replica of the physical body. This is the part of a human that, at death, will depart the body, and we will know a person as we knew them on earth as the spirit is the mirror reflection of that person. It is also interesting to note how all emotions, whether pain, sorrow, fear, anxiety — both negative and positive feelings, can be sensed as emerging from the area of the belly.

The soul appears to be linked with the brain, the mind, the reasoning process, and the five senses. It is what connects the physical man with the spiritual man and is the lifeforce within the body. The human soul can be either carnal or spiritual. Outside of the human body, the soul and spirit maintain all five senses: hearing, seeing, smelling, tasting, and touching, as indicated in the narrative recorded by Luke in chapter 16. The rich man's soul and spirit were in hell. He recalled details of his past life, not feeding a poor man, the fact that he had five brothers still living, and how he could feel the pain of being tormented in the flame (Luke 16:19-31). Abraham told this eternally lost soul, "Remember in your lifetime..." (Luke 16:25). Total recall of the past was evident in this statement. The spirit of the man retained the same appearance as his physical body. However, his soul had the senses to feel and recall life details.

The physical body is the only part that is affected by the death process, as it will return to the dust of the earth. The soul and spirit of each person will never be destroyed and will live in one of two worlds for eternity.

CHAPTER TEN

WHEN GOD CAN'T FIND YOUR NAME IN THE BOOK OF LIFE

Heaven is a literal place, perhaps a large planet, with countless angels, various types of mountains, crystal clear rivers, flowers, and animals (including horses). It has beautiful trees, featuring the famous tree of life (Rev. 22:2). In fact, the natural beauty covering the earth is patterned after, and a reflection of, the original beauty which fills the scenery in the third heaven. One of the most interesting facts of this upper celestial kingdom is how earthly information is stored in heavenly books. One day, it will all be made public in one of two places. Either at the Judgment Seat of Christ, a heavenly judgment and reward ceremony for believers (2 Cor. 5:10), or the Great White Throne judgment (Rev. 20:11-15), a frightful judgment reserved for the lost souls of eons past. This includes Satan, fallen angels, and spirit rebels who died without a covenant with God during the Old Testament era. It also includes the unbelievers from Christ's time up to the time of this judgment.

The Scripture identifies five distinct books, each designated for recording specific, detailed information about each person who was born and lived on earth. Just as the local, state, and federal governments have collected personal information on the details of personal conversations and transactions, God has a recording and retrieval system unmatched by even the greatest tech companies.

Psalms 69:28 and 139:16 speaks of a "Book of the Living." While there are differences of opinions as to the type of information stored in this particular heavenly book, some suggest that it holds the earthly details of a person's life. David wrote that God knew him, including each bodily part, and recorded those specifics in His book, *before* he was born on earth. Psalms 139:15-16 may allude to this heavenly book of the living. There are a few Jewish rabbis who identify this book as "The Book of Destiny." According to some rabbinical theories, this book details God's life-destiny purposes and assignments for His people.

The second and most alluded to book in Scripture linked to believers is called, "The Book of Life" (Phil. 4:3; Rev. 3:5). This is what I term the heavenly registry or the "roll call of the redeemed." When a person truly repents of their sins, entering a redemptive covenant with God through Christ, their name is inscribed in this book. This is the book Christ referred to when His disciples were rejoicing because they had authority over evil spirits. Jesus said, "...rejoice... because your names are written in heaven" (Luke 10:20). Your name being inscribed in this book gives you access to the eternal city of God and eternal life. I call this book, the registry of heaven.

One unique book mentioned only once in Scripture is the "Book of Tears." David wrote, "...put my tears in thy bottle are they not in thy book" (Psa. 56:8). An ancient custom during times of grief was to place the tears of the grieving in a small glass bottle called a "tear bottle." The top of the bottle was sealed with wax, preventing the precious tears from escaping or evaporating. David knew God kept a heavenly book recording the number of tears he had shed. This may seem strange to us. However, Christ also indicated that the very hairs on a person's head are numbered (Luke 12:7). This tear book reveals God's love and watchfulness for us when we experience grief or sorrow. He counts hairs and records tears.

The fourth heavenly book is called the "Book of Remembrance." This book is referenced in one Biblical passage penned in Malachi 3:16-17. This is perhaps the most mysterious book mentioned among the heavenly registries. According to Scripture, there are names recorded in this book, honoring those who are givers, tithers, and fear the name of the Lord (see Malachi 3). Malachi indicates that those whose names are inscribed in this book belong to the Lord. They will be His on the day He "makes up His jewels," and He will spare them on the day of trouble, the way a father spares his son. Acts 10:1-4 confirms this book's existence when the angel tells Cornelius that his "prayers and financial giving" (alms-KJV), had "come up before God as a memorial." The information in the Book of Remembrance came up before God, was recognized, and honored in God's presence. The Lord was sending Cornelius special blessings for his obedience and faithfulness. The word "memorial" (Acts 10) in the Hebrew language has the same meaning as the word "remembrance." This Book of Remembrance records the names of those who are obedient and faithful to God. This book is also important, according to the context in Malachi chapters 3 and 4, as when the day of trouble comes (or the Great Tribulation), and God gathers His jewels (the righteous), He will "spare" those whose names are in this book, from the future judgment because their names were inscribed in this special book (see Malachi chapters 3 and 4).

The fifth book of importance is, in reality, a *series of books* that catalog the works and various deeds that were performed by all people living on earth. Rewards will be presented to the faithful, or rewards will be withheld at the heavenly tribunals based upon what a person *did or did not do* on earth. John, in Revelation, describes one of the two judgments as follows:

"And I saw the dead, small and great, stand before God; and the books were opened: and another book was opened, which is the Book of Life: and the dead were judged out of those things which were written in the books, according to their works."

— Revelation 20:12

In Hebrews 12:23, the inspired writer noted the following:

"To the general assembly and the church of the firstborn who are registered in heaven, to God the Judge of all, and the spirits of just men made perfect."

— Hebrews 12:23 (NKJV)

The King James Version says, "written in heaven." The word "written" is used in the 1611 version of the New Testament, one hundred thirty-two times. The word "written" used in Hebrews 12:23 is slightly different in Greek than the normal word used for writing something down on paper. This word is *apographo* and alludes to enrolling or entering something into records. It refers to entering a person's name, property information, income tax, and legal information on official government registries and ledgers. This indicates that our eternal access to heaven is a legal matter based upon the blood covenant of Christ and not just a spiritual blessing.

REGISTRIES IN THE ANCIENT EMPIRES

The area of ancient Mesopotamia was the original home of Abraham. This early patriarch departed from Ur of the Chaldees to move to his new homeland of Canaan (later called Israel). Mesopotamia is where some of the earliest civilizations and languages originated. Years ago, in this region, an amazing discovery was made. Clay tablets called the *Tablets of Transgression,* and the *Tablets of Destiny* were found.

Scholars interpreting these tablets note that the tablets were religious in nature. The two tablets are similar to what we read in Scripture, referring to the names being "inscribed" or "blotted out" of the Book of Life (Rev. 3:5). If a man's name was written on the Tablets of Transgression for something evil he had done, then his name was blotted out of the Tablets of Destiny. The ancient belief among those living in that region was that each year, the gods gathered in a heavenly "fate-room." Every man's life was recorded in books, and yearly decisions were made as to the fate of each person. This idea may have spread to various early religions. From the time of Adam, for the first 1,800 years, men spoke one language until the languages were divided at the Tower of Babel (see Gen. 11).

From a Jewish perspective, Israel's sixth appointed season is the yearly Day of Atonement (Lev. 23:27-28). On the seventh month, and the tenth day, God set this one day aside to determine the spiritual fate of each individual, including the spiritual fate of the nation of Israel. Their destiny is based upon their repentance, or the lack thereof. An example of this is found in the book of Daniel when King Nebuchadnezzar was warned to repent of his pride or suffer a severe judgment from God. The king refused to follow Daniel's admonition, and exactly twelve months later, he suffered a horrendous mental breakdown and ended up living like a wild beast in the wilderness for seven years (Dan. 4:17). One full year was extended to the king as a "space" to repent (note Rev. 2:21). However, he failed to do so, sealing his fate as decreed by the heavenly watchers.

THE NEO-ASSYRIAN REGISTRIES

Books being used to record personal information on individuals continued into the Neo-Assyrian time. Books were used to record both the good and the bad deeds that people committed. Names could be placed in registries and later marked through. The names of bad people (criminals) were removed, and the names of the good citizens remained.

The idea of specific *registries* recording names was not just a Biblical revelation that was revealed to Moses, the prophets, and apostles but was also practiced at the temple in Jerusalem among the priesthood. Judea was known as the most religious region in Israel, being the land grant given to the tribe of Judah. When the ten tribes of Israel were taken captive by the Assyrians, the inhabitants of both Judah and Benjamin remained at Israel's southern boundary. The temple of Solomon in Jerusalem was built on the land grant between the tribes of Judah and Benjamin.

In the temple registries, the names of fully qualified Jewish citizens were recorded. One of the most important books was maintained within the temple itself, which was the registry of all the priests serving at the temple. When a man wanted to be a priest, his qualifications had to be reviewed. He underwent a comprehensive process, including proving his background and undergoing a detailed physical examination to determine if he had any physical defects that would disqualify him. He also underwent questioning to determine his spiritual knowledge. Once he was approved, he was given a white priestly robe, and his *name was inscribed* in the priestly registry.

The Jewish Mishnah reminds its readers about their recorded deeds:

> "Know what is above thee: a seeing eye, a hearing ear, and thy deeds written in a book."
>
> – The Mishnah; Avot 2:1

One of the Jewish prayers prayed from Trumpets to the Day of Atonement is:

"Remember us unto life, O king who delights in life, and inscribe us in the Book of Life, for thine own sake, O God of life."

Included in the heavenly books are the actions of wicked individuals. In Acts 19:23-41, Paul was ministering in Ephesus, where those operating a lucrative idol-making business accused Paul of blaspheming the gods of the city. One man, a coppersmith named Alexander, instigated an uprising, leading a mob revolt against Paul, causing him much harm. Years later, In Paul's final epistle, he wrote:

"Alexander the coppersmith did me much harm. May the Lord repay him according to his works. You also must beware of him, for he has greatly resisted our words."

– 2 TIM. 4:14-15 (NKJV)

Paul wrote in 1 Timothy 1:20 for church members to turn Alexander over to Satan so that he would learn not to blaspheme. When Paul wrote "the Lord reward him," this could refer to God bringing earthly judgment upon this evil man or could refer to confronting him at the heavenly judgment where he will receive what Peter termed, "the reward of unrighteousness" (2 Pet. 2:13). The final reward for unrighteousness is when the wicked are eternally separated from God in the Lake of Fire (Rev. 20:14).

Certain heavenly registries record information on all living humans, including detailed data related to their earthly life, behavior, and actions. Solomon noted this when he wrote:

"For God shall bring every work into judgment, with every secret thing, whether it be good, or whether it be evil."

– ECCLESIASTES 12:14

THE LAMB'S BOOK OF LIFE

At the Great White Throne judgment, the heavenly books will be opened. As noted earlier, one of those books located in this celestial repository is called "the Book of Life" (Rev. 21:27).

> "And I saw the dead, small and great, stand before God; and the books were opened: and another book was opened, which is the book of life: and the dead were judged out of those things which were written in the books, according to their works."
>
> — Revelation 20:12

> "And whosoever was not found written in the book of life was cast into the lake of fire."
>
> — Revelation 20:15

The most frightening statement an individual could ever hear would be Christ, looking into their eyes on judgment day saying, "I never knew you: depart from me" (Matt. 7:23). This statement initiates eternal separation from God. When a person's name is *not found* penned in the Book of Life, it indicates they never repented of their sins, never entering into a redemptive covenant with Jesus Christ. On the other hand, there will be a different announcement proclaimed at the Judgment Seat of Christ for those who are in covenant with Him. The Lord will welcome those into His kingdom saying, "Well done, good and faithful servant... enter into the joy of the Lord" (Matt. 25:23). The word "good" in this passage can allude to being beneficial, meaning your life was a benefit for the kingdom of God. The difference between the two states of "well done" or "depart" will be what is written in the heavenly books. May no one reading *this book* ever hear the words, *"Your name is not in the Book of Life."*

BLOTTING OUT NAMES OR SINS

The word "blot" is a word used in both testaments (Exod. 32:32; Rev. 3:5). The Scripture indicates that the names inscribed in the Book of Life can also be blotted out. The word blot is also used in references where David prayed for God to "blot out his transgressions" (Psa. 51:1) and to "blot out his iniquities" (Psa. 51:9). This same theme is carried over into the New Testament, where Peter told the Jewish audience on Pentecost, "Repent therefore and be converted that your sins may be blotted out..." (Acts 3:19). The term *"blotted out"* here in Greek *is exaleipho*, and refers to smearing out, to obliviate, or to erase. There are four meanings in Greek for this word. One means to cover with lime and whitewash plaster, which would hide and cover anything written on it. Another meaning is to erase, wipe out, and completely remove. This is what God does to your sins when you repent. God revealed to Isaiah that He would "blot out your transgressions, and not remember your sins" (Isa. 43:25).

God blots out sins. Why, how, and when are names blotted out of this heavenly Book of Life? As a child, I was confused with this concept as I assumed (based on early full-gospel preaching) that if I sinned, my name was automatically removed from the Book of Life. I visualized a huge angel with a giant pencil and eraser that spent his time inscribing, then erasing, inscribing, then erasing my name anytime I sinned or disobeyed, as in my mind, any sin instantly forfeited my name in the divine registry.

Years later, I read in Revelation of a female teacher in the church at Thyatira, who was seducing numerous men within the church, sexually, and through false doctrine. Instead of God instantly killing her, permanently removing this seducer from the church, Christ told John, "I have given her a space to repent" (Rev. 2:21). The word *"space"* is the Greek word *"chronos"* and refers to a specific space of time. God had set a time frame, waiting to see the response of the woman. If her heart and actions did not change, God announced He would release a serious tribulation against her (Rev. 2:23).

Christ informed Simon Peter that Satan was setting him up for a trap that he would fall into. Instead of warning Peter of the dangers (his name could be blotted out), Christ said to him that He had prayed for him that his "faith would not fail" (Luke 22:32). Jesus then said, "When you are converted, strengthen your brethren." (Luke 22:32). The word "converted" means to *revert back* or to *"come again."* Christ knew two things would happen: Peter would fail the test, and Peter would repent and come back to the ministry.

Biblically, if a born-again believer is overtaken in a fault (Gal.6:1) or falls into the trap of temptation leading to sin, their name is not *instantly* blotted out of the book. There is a "space" for repentance provided by God. This space is to convict someone of their spiritual or moral conditions. He observes the persons choice to either continue in their own rebellion and disobedience or turn to Him with a repentant heart asking for freedom and forgiveness. The question that has been asked for centuries is *when* is a person's name actually blotted out of the Book of Life?

MOSES — BLOT MY NAME OUT

The answer might be concealed in a statement Moses made to the Lord after departing Egypt. The Israelites took their gold jewelry, constructed a gold calf, and worshipped it as an idol. God's wrath was kindled, and He said to Moses that He was prepared to "blot the names" of all of Israel out of His heavenly book. Moses made emergency intercession and requested to the Lord, "If thou wilt forgive their sin; and if not, blot me out of the book which you have written" (Exod. 32:32-33 NKJV). Moses recorded more detail of this incident, including God's back-up plan in Deuteronomy 9:14 (NKJV):

"Let me alone, that I may destroy them, and blot out their name from under heaven: and I will make of thee a nation mightier and greater than they."

After carefully examining this verse, God offered two possibilities at once. First, to literally wipe out the entire nation of Israel that departed out of Egypt. That would have been 600,000 men, not counting women and children (this would have been through a sudden plague), leaving Moses as the lone survivor. Part two included a plan for Moses to father a second nation of Hebrews. God was also prepared to "blot out their names," the names of the entire Hebrew nation in the wilderness, all of which were in the heavenly registry. When examining this text, I was made aware that the blotting out process would have occurred at the *same time as the death* of the Israelites.

There have been many different religions, not just Christianity, where the followers relate a story of clinically dying, seeing a "great light," and entering a long type tunnel. They describe a feeling of being "judged" by this light. Some say it was God. Others who were Biblically uninformed called this light some type of "supernatural being." There are also stories of some non-Christians that returned to life or were resuscitated in a hospital, that never passed beyond the tunnel of judging light.

It is possible that the "blotting out process" actually occurs at the moment of a person's death. If a person dies in their sins, having once known the Lord and turned away from him, never repenting, the person's name can be blotted out of the Book of Life. The individual who has "overcome" the world, the flesh, and the devil, is ensured a place in heaven as their name remains inscribed in the Book of Life:

"He that over cometh, the same shall be clothed in white raiment; and I will not blot out his name out of the book of life, but I will confess his name before my Father, and before his angels."

— Revelation 3:5

The Scripture indicates, "it is appointed unto men once to die, but after this the judgment" (Heb. 9:27). The New Testament indicates there is a judgment of the "living and the dead." The living being those who will be caught up to meet the Lord in the air at the Rapture (1 Thess. 4:16-17), and the "dead" referring to the "dead in Christ" who will be raised at the same return we call the "Rapture." This judgment is the Judgment Seat of Christ.

The Greek word for judgment in Hebrews 9:27 is "krisis," and is a common word for any type of tribunal or legal trial that a person must undergo to determine innocence or guilt. It may be possible that when a person's death appointment arrives, and the spirit exits the body, then God, the judge of all, determines if the person's name remains in the book or is blotted out. In my study of near-death experiences, most people describe the same four or five incidents occurring within seconds. There is a sudden complete darkness, often followed by a strange, loud buzzing sound in the ears. Within seconds, a white or multi-colored light as bright as the sun becomes visible. The individual describes the sensation of being released from their body, moving at great speeds toward the light. At this moment, many hear voices, see faces, or sense that the light is searching them deeply, judging them in some manner. As for the light, we read that God "…hath immortality, dwelling in the light that no man can approach…" (1 Tim. 6:16).

For centuries, there has been a theological debate over what I often term conditional and unconditional eternal security. This is not the place to debate the differences between these two beliefs as both have their strong points and specific Scripture references. My emphasis here is to show that a name, under certain conditions, can be blotted out of the Book of Life. Remember, this is the book that a name must remain in to have eternal life with Christ throughout eternity.

I teach believers to remain faithful, keep a repentant heart and spirit, and if they sin against God or man, be swift to repent, and ask for forgiveness. Keep your spirit clean of offenses, and if you live by the Word of God with a repentant heart, your name is secure.

CHAPTER ELEVEN

DO ALL CHILDREN GO TO HEAVEN?

In 1979, in Danville, Virginia, a young mother was in a rush to get to work. She got in her car and backed out of her driveway like any other day. She didn't know that her five-year-old daughter had been playing outside and was hiding behind her car. As she was backing out, she ran over her beautiful child, instantly killing her precious girl. I preached a revival at her church shortly after this tragedy occurred. I saw the pain and grief in her mother's face, as she asked herself *why* this happened, and could she have done something to prevent it? *The mother was living on earth while her heart was in heaven.*

During a five-week revival at Pastor Jentezen Franklin's church (Free Chapel) in Gainesville, Georgia, the church received a call informing them of a horrible accident involving a family of the church. A garbage truck lowered its metal forks and struck a van with a mother and her three children inside. Two of her three children, including her infant, were killed. Suddenly, the mother found that her heart was now split between a child on the earth and two whose innocent spirits were now in the third heaven.

A child is expected to grow, experience life, and outlive their parents. Parents aren't meant to live longer than their children. However, for some unexplainable reason, this normal life-cycle pattern becomes interrupted when something life-threatening happens. Whether it be a physical disease, an accident, or a sudden tragedy that stops a child's journey, it is life-altering. The comforting news for a Christian parent is that in eternity, no children are separated from God. *They are all residents of the heavenly paradise.*

THE 5-YEAR-OLD WHO WENT TO HEAVEN

I was told a story by a young lady that I met while preaching in Louisville, Kentucky. When she was age five, she visited heaven. Her family was living in Tyler, Texas. It was the month of May, and it was very hot, so her parents took her swimming at their pastor's house. The adults were in the house when suddenly they heard a scream. They ran outside to find her lying face down in the pool. She was using a floaty, but the rope had come untied. This young lady said she remembered seeing the steps under the water as she went up and down a few times, taking in water, and then suddenly everything went black. The family began praying and called 911. The rescue team worked on reviving her until she threw up water and came back to life. She was wrapped in a blanket and sent to the emergency room. After several tests and spending half the day in the hospital, she was sent home.

On the way home, she told her parents that she had been taken to heaven from the pool! When she was blacking out, she saw an angel come into the water. He took her by her hand and carried her through an open black sky. He then sat her at the entrance of a gate. The gate was white, and there were two huge angels with swords. She saw a street that looked like gold, but it was clear, and she looked down and could see herself. A wall connected to the gate from either side, and she could not see the end of the wall. It was dark above and behind her but light where she was. When she looked through the floor, she could actually see the pool that was back on earth and saw people trying to revive her. She had on a garment that was soft that she described as feeling like velvet, but it wasn't velvet, it was different. She observed angels with wings, some that were short, and others that were long.

Christ Himself came to her and took her. She said He had dark hair, dark eyes, and a dark tanned skin tone. She would think something, and He would respond, without saying anything. Being from Texas, the grass where she lived had little sand burs that would stick to your feet when you walked on the grass barefooted. She walked on the grass in heaven, and the Lord read her thoughts as she thought to herself that there were no grass stickers in heaven.

It was then that she saw something amazing. In the children's paradise, there was a lake with flowers swimming in it, and if you picked them up, they were immediately dry. There were all sorts of animals that the children could play with. She saw houses that were small with trees. She saw children playing in areas with other children their ages. She saw her mother's mother in a beautiful house. She had never met nor seen this person before she died! She was making what appeared to be a beautiful salad made of all types of fruit. There was a big letter C on the outside of her house. The young lady didn't know this, but her earthly name was Mrs. Cox. She told her, "Tell your mom that I love her!" On earth, her mother had never heard her mom say, "I love you." I heard this story related to me personally by the young girl who experienced it.

I WILL SEE THEM AGAIN

David's adultery led to Bathsheba becoming pregnant with his child. The infant died seven days after its birth. David fasted for one week in hopes that God would heal his sick son. When the infant breathed its last breath, the Bible records David's response:

"So David arose from the ground, washed and anointed himself, and changed his clothes; and he went into the house of the LORD and worshiped. Then he went to his own house; and when he requested, they set food before him, and he ate. Then his servants said to him, "What is this that you have done? You fasted and wept for the child while he was alive, but when the child died, you arose and ate food. And he said, "While the child was alive, I fasted and wept; for I said, 'Who can tell whether the LORD will be gracious to me, that the child may live?' But now he is dead; why should I fast? Can I bring him back again? I shall go to him, but he shall not return to me."

– 2 SAMUEL 12:20-23 (NKJV)

David understood, at the moment of death, his son's eternal soul and spirit were absent from its tiny body and were actively alive, dwelling in the eternal realm. Using David's revelation as the foundation, I will explore the Biblical teaching concerning infants and children in heaven, and why at death, these innocent ones are taken into the presence of God in heaven.

CHILDREN ARE IN THE KINGDOM

Our interpretation of children going to heaven is based on five unique statements made by Christ concerning children. In Matthew 18:3, Jesus spoke to an adult audience about entering the kingdom of heaven. We read:

"And said, Verily I say unto you, Except ye be converted, and become as little children, ye shall not enter into the kingdom of heaven."

– MATTHEW 18:3

The word *children* here in Greek is *paidion* and alludes to a half-grown male or female. It refers to a child that is still at an immature level and is dependent upon its parents. The next verse, Matthew 18:4, reveals the context of Christ's statement that men should "humble themselves as a little child" to enter the kingdom. Pride and arrogance prevent many from repenting and turning from their sins as they believe they are as "good as anyone else," and don't need redemption. However, a child's heart is often tender and sensitive, as witnessed when being rebuked by a parent or guardian. They often cry and become sorrowful.

Jesus, in a later discourse, revealed that children are part of the kingdom. On one occasion, parents were lined up with their children seeking Christ to lay hands upon them to bless them. The disciples viewed this as a distraction and began rebuking the parents. Jesus issued this response which countered the disciple's resistance by saying:

> "Then were there brought unto him little children, that he should put his hands on them, and pray: and the disciples rebuked them. But Jesus said, Suffer little children, and forbid them not, to come unto me: for of such is the kingdom of heaven."
>
> – MATTHEW 19:13-14

The phrase *"little children"* is a phrase alluding to infants, or very young children, as indicated in Luke 18:15, "they brought unto him infants…" The verse can actually read, "the kingdom of heaven is composed of such," referring to small children or infants. The way infants make up the kingdom of heaven would be when they pass away (such as David's infant son) through death on earth, which releases their eternal spirits to enter the heavenly paradise.

Christ's love for children was so passionate. He gave a warning to anyone who willfully offended a child. This serious injunction is found in Matthew 18:5-6:

"And whoso shall receive one such little child in my name receiveth me. But whoso shall offend one of these little ones which believe in me, it were better for him that a millstone were hanged about his neck, and that he were drowned in the depth of the sea."

The phrase "little ones" used here in Greek is the word *mikros* and refers to one that is small in size. The word is used in six New Testament verses, and all six references refer to a small child. The word "offend" means "to entice, trip up, or entice to sin." This warning is addressed to adults who would cause a child to turn from their faith or lead a child or a young person to sin. This warning would apply to men or women who physically or sexually abuse a child, including drug dealers who target youth, enticing them toward illegal drugs. It would also include those connected with alcoholic beverages who market their products to youth, whose indulgence leads many to become drunk, and some, alcoholics. In our time, it would also be a warning to producers in the pornographic industry using the internet, targeting children in their pre-teens to become addicted to pornography. Enticing, encouraging, or opening a door for a child to sin is a high-level transgression, and Christ pointed out that it would be better for the offender to "tie a mill-stone around his neck and jump into the sea." A millstone is a large, round, hand-cut rock, weighing hundreds of pounds (some weigh over a ton) used for grinding grains. In ancient Syria and Greece, one death penalty for certain crimes was to drown a person by tying a weight around their neck. Thus, this strange form of penalty was not a new idea that Christ introduced. If a person committed a serious atrocity that affected the community, this penalty was used. Christ takes offending a child seriously.

Children are dearly beloved of God and are assigned their own angels that are continually ministering before God's throne. Recorded in Matthew 18:10, Christ revealed this truth:

> "Take heed that ye despise not one of these little ones; for I say unto you, that in heaven their angels do always behold the face of my Father which is in heaven."

Notice the phrase, "their angels." The word "their" makes the phrase personal. We could say, "the angels that guard and watch over children continually see God's face in heaven." Based on a vision given to the Prophet Micaiah, the heavenly courtroom, where God sits upon His throne, is surrounded by countless angels standing on His left and right side. These ministering angels are sent to earth with specific assignments (see 2 Chronicles 18:18-22). On this occasion, one of the heavenly messengers set up King Ahab by using the evil king's false prophets to encourage him to go to battle. They told him he would win the war. However, God's plan was that the king would be slain in battle, which he was. Christ's implication is that angels observe children and watch their actions, especially any bad behavior that adults initiate or create toward them. These guardian angels can report to God, and God's anger toward the abuser can release a decision of judgment against those who verbally, physically, or emotionally do harm to a child.

One of the strongest verses that confirm it is the will of God for infants and innocent children to enter heaven is the following statement, *"Children are not to perish.* Again, Matthew's Gospel records Christ's amazing statement:

"Even so it is not the will of your Father which is in heaven, that one of these little ones should perish."

– Matthew 18:14

The keyword in this verse is *"perish."* The word perish is used thirty times in thirty verses in the New Testament, and in all references, except ten, it is the same Greek word *apollummi* and can be translated as "to fully destroy, to perish or to lose, both literally and figuratively." The word is used when Christ said, "Except you repent you shall all likewise perish" (Luke 13:3), and if we believe in Him, we "shall not perish, but have everlasting life" (John 3:16). Peter said it was not God's will that "any perish, but that all should come to repentance" (2 Pet. 3:9). Thus, in numerous passages, the word "perish" alludes to dying lost and separated from God. The Bible affirms that a lost person will spend eternity in the Lake of Fire far from God's presence.

It is clear from Matthew 18:14 that it is not God's will for any "little one" (child) to *perish* or die in a *spiritually lost condition*, separated from God. Children are part of God's heavenly kingdom. The reason is, as infants and children, they know neither good nor evil, as indicated in several Old Testaments verses. According to John 10:28, if we believe in Christ, we are given eternal life and shall "never perish."

THE INNOCENCE OF A CHILD

Scriptures indicate that a child enters the womb *spiritually neutral*, as they have done neither good nor bad. Paul alludes to this in his epistle to the Romans:

"And not only this; but when Rebecca also had conceived by one, even by our father Isaac; For the children being not yet born, neither having done any good or evil, that the purpose of God according to election might stand, not of works, but of him that calleth."

— Romans 9:10-11

Rebecca was the wife of Isaac. She was pregnant with twins: Jacob and Esau. As infants, they were both innocent from acts of disobedience. Things changed as they grew into men. Scripture reveals the deceptive nature of Jacob. Esau, during a weak moment, traded away his birthright to his brother for a bowl of lentil soup, despising his birthright (see Genesis 25). Children cannot establish a value system of right and wrong as an infant. Their value and belief ideology develop over time based upon their culture, upbringing, and family influence.

After Noah's flood, God noted that *all men* have an evil imagination that begins during their youth (Gen. 8:21). This is identified by rabbis as "the evil inclination," meaning an inner tendency leaning toward rebellion, stubbornness, and disobedience. These tendencies impact our views of others. They cause us to pull away from God's laws and commandments. Isaiah, in a Messianic prophecy (see Isa. 7:14), noted that the future Messiah would have a sense of discernment, "that he may know to refuse the evil and choose the good" (Isa.7:15).

When Israel departed from Egypt, they fell into unbelief, causing the older generation to not enter into the Promised Land. God, however, allowed the *children* born in the wilderness to the unbelieving parents, to grow up and enter the land of promise. God's instructions were:

"Moreover, your little ones and your children, who you say will be victims, who today have no knowledge of good and evil, they shall go in there; to them I will give it, and they shall possess it."

– DEUTERONOMY 1:39 NKJV

Here again, it is noted that small children have no knowledge of good or evil. It is when children mature physically, emotionally, and mentally, that they can be taught the difference between good and evil, right and wrong. On their own, they have no internal knowledge of good and evil. A child may take another's toy, not understanding it does not belong to them unless they are taught the difference. When my son was four, he overheard some cursing and began repeating the words he heard. We had to teach him not to say those words even though he didn't understand. To him, they were just words. As children become adults, there is a *sin nature* that can be fed through the pressure of temptation. The rebellious inclination will emerge and must be dealt with. However, children are innocent until taught, and this leads us to a term called "the age of accountability."

THE BAR MITZVAH AND BAT MITZVAH

There have been lengthy discussions among scholars as to when a child becomes accountable for their own actions. This is what we call the "age of accountability?" Among devout Jews, there is a celebration known as "Bar Mitzva" and "Bat Mitzva." The word "bar" is a Jewish-Babylonian-Aramaic word meaning "son" while "bat" in Hebrew means "daughter." The word mitzvah means "commandment" or "law" (the plural is mitzvot). Among religious Jews, when a son or daughter reaches their thirteenth birthday, a unique religious ceremony is conducted by the family and rabbis, initiating a Jewish boy or girl into the age of accountability. This ceremony indicates they are ready to participate in personally observing the teaching and precepts of the Torah and Judaism. At the age of 12 for a girl and 13 for a boy, the responsibility of sin, personal actions, and choices are now placed upon them instead of their parents who have been responsible for their spiritual and moral upbringing. After participating in this ceremony, the child takes on the moral and spiritual responsibility for their own choices and decisions.

Luke recorded an interesting narrative when he wrote about the time Mary, Joseph, Jesus, and His relatives traveled to Jerusalem to celebrate a Jewish festival. Because this story involved Christ's entire family, the festival may have been the Festival of Tabernacles. According to some scholars, this festival would have fallen on or near Christ's birthday, which was during the fall festival months. When His parents could not find Him among the caravan, they returned to the temple in Jerusalem, discovering the twelve-year-old Jesus sitting with the scribes and scholars listening to their discussions and asking questions. When they asked Him why He was missing from the caravan returning home, He answered them, "I must be about my Father's business" (Luke 2:42-49).

Jesus understood that His family had been responsible, up until that moment, for His upbringing. However, He was arriving at the age in which He would personally seek the will and desires of His heavenly Father, including taking personal responsibility for His own actions.

During this age of accountability ceremony, the earthly father gives thanks to God that he is no longer punished for the sins of his son (or daughter). One of the Old Testament principles is that the sins of the fathers can be laid upon the third and fourth generation of those who disobey God (Exod. 20:5; 34:7). It is interesting that the bar and bat mitzvahs also coincide with the age of physical puberty.

The transition period from twelve to thirteen could very well be the *average age of accountability* for most sons and daughters. That's the age the mind, body, and spirit start to mature from a child to a young adult. During the teenage years, most youths begin to view themselves as young adults and begin to take upon themselves more responsibilities, such as driving, a job, and preparing for college.

TAKING SUFFERING CHILDREN TO HEAVEN

One of the common questions posed by secular unbelievers who challenge God's goodness is, "If there is a God and He is allegedly good, then why are children suffering?" There is no set answer that can satisfy the more critical, philosophical seeker. However, I must note four observations that do come into play when considering this question.

First, there are millions of children born in nations that are steeped with serious superstition and idolatry. False gods carved of wood and stone hold more value than a human life. In some nations, the idol god or goddess is given money and food while family members suffer and go without. In other idolatrous countries, the belief in reincarnation makes it impossible to slaughter an animal. Their religious beliefs forbid such action, considering a person who has passed away may "reincarnate" in the form of an animal. All animals must be preserved. We cannot blame these religious ideas and self-imposed poverty upon the true God. The blame should fall on humanity's man-made religious superstitions.

The second reason children suffer is that they are born in countries ruled by wicked dictators. For example, in the days of Iraqi dictator Saddam Hussein, this madman was labeled by his own people as the "Butcher of Baghdad," torturing and murdering tens of thousands of his own people. He initiated a long nine-year war against neighboring Iran. The land between the two countries concealed hidden land mines to prevent Iraqi troops from crossing. To clear these deadly mines, Saddam hung huge plastic keys around the necks of children, instructing them to run across the minefield. He told them that if they died, the plastic key would unlock the entrance to the gates of paradise. The children were given no choice but to follow the dictates of this madman. God cannot be blamed for the actions of evil men who reject God's choices for their own abuse of power.

Some nations have their own national bondages that manipulate children for their own perverted pleasures. Throughout Europe and the Philippines, there are an estimated 28 million children and youth forced into sex slavery. Some teenage girls are forced to have sex 100 times a day. This kind of abuse and perversion are forbidden by the Almighty. Eventually, severe judgment will come on the leaders and the nations. Should they not receive their penalty on earth, their eternal damnation is set after they die an earthly death. Paul wrote, "Some men's sins are open beforehand, going before to judgment; and some men they follow after" (1 Tim. 5:24). This means some men will experience exposure of their evil in this life (such as Ben Laden, Saddam Hussein, and Hitler), and others will have their evil exposed at the judgment.

Thirdly, children suffer as a result of natural disasters such as droughts and famines. Every five seconds, a child dies. When you do the math, twelve children die every minute, 720 in an hour, and 17,280 a day. In the African nation of Niger, 3.6 million people do not have enough food. Globally, every minute, twenty people die from starvation and disease. Presently, this earth in under a Genesis 3:17 "curse" resulting from Adam's fall. Romans 8:22 indicates that creation is presently groaning and travailing. Earthquakes, famines, and pestilences are a part of the early birth pangs experienced at the time of the end (Matt. 24:7-8). During earthquakes, tsunamis, hurricanes, volcanic eruptions, and other natural disasters, children are often caught in the crisis and suffer as much as the adults. Again, this is not the fault of God. This is the result of disasters that cannot be controlled or prevented by human ingenuity. Jesus said that "the sun rises on both good and evil and it rains upon the just and the unjust" (Matt. 5:45).

At times, the decisions made by parents or by a wicked generation impact future generations. Moses warned that the "iniquities of the fathers" could be passed down to the third and fourth generation of them that hate the Lord (Exod. 34:7; Num. 14:18; Deut. 5:9). In two of these warnings, Israel had sinned, and God was warning them that their sins would not only impact them, but unless they repented, it would affect their children and their children's children.

The best example of this is when Jesus stood before Pilate, who, three times, declared Jesus "innocent," hoping the multitude would seek His release and not His death. Pilate's wife experienced a troubling dream and warned Pilate not to harm Christ (Matt. 27:19). Pilate knew the law of Moses. He knew that anyone guilty of shedding innocent blood would not only be themselves cursed, but a curse would also be placed upon their land. In the law, if a stranger is found dead near a city, the elders must slay a heifer and *wash their hands* over the head of the slain animal, indicating they are not guilty of its death (see Deut. 21:1-6). Pilate publicly stood at a washbasin, washed his hands, and said he was "innocent of the blood of this just person" (Matt. 27:24). He was partially enacting the law of release from the shedding of innocent blood as instructed in the Torah, in Deuteronomy 21. He washed his hands from the guilt of shedding innocent blood. The devout Jewish religious leaders understood what Pilate was doing, and yet they verbally released this dangerous proclamation:

> "And all of the people answered and said, His blood be on us and our children."
>
> – MATTHEW 27:25 (NKJV)

By making this decree, and by permitting innocent blood to be spilled in Jerusalem, the religious leaders and people placed a self-curse upon their own children. Jesus knew this was coming and warned in Matthew 23 that His generation would be judged for shedding the blood of the prophets and righteous men. Christ also revealed that He would have gathered Jerusalem together as a hen does her chicks under her protective wing, but they would not permit it. Jesus was indicating that He could release a level of protection to the children of these rebellious leaders, but instead, their children, in one generation, would see the desolation of Jerusalem (see Matthew 23:35-38) because of the sins of their fathers.

The fourth reason some children suffer is because of the decisions made by their parents. When parents become alcoholics, it destroys the love and income needed to build a strong family. Drug addiction often opens the door for children to be taken from their parents and placed in foster care. Abuse can also lead a child into the system, instead of being with their biological parents. It is the same scenario with addicts as it is with those spending time in prison. Decisions to commit certain crimes can lead to a parent being incarcerated for a period of time, causing them to be separated from their children. These negative choices are *not being caused by a lack of the Lord's love,* but by the sins and disobedience of those to whom He gave power and authority to choose.

These key elements, worshipping national idols, living in a nation with a dangerous dictator, natural disasters, national bondages such as illegal drug infestations, and the bad choices of parents, cause pain in the life of children throughout the world.

Years ago, a tragic tsunami struck in Indonesia. It took the lives of tens of thousands of people, not just in Indonesia, but in other nations as well. I was troubled as to the number of children this disaster claimed. After praying, I realized that God, at times, will allow infants and children to pass (at an early age) to keep them from sin, idolatry, physical dangers, and the sexual abuse that would become a part of their life. Death was not a judgment, but it was mercy upon their souls to bring them to heaven.

THE DEATH OF A TEENAGER

Often times, a tragic accident or sickness will take the life of a strong Christian teenager. At the funeral, many questions remain unanswered, specifically, "Why did God allow a person so young to die?" Could God not have prevented it?" It would require a large book to hold all the theological discourses had throughout many centuries, all of which have attempted to draw a conclusion to this question.

Perhaps Solomon was meditating on this question when he wrote:

"Although all have sinned, be not wicked overmuch or willfully, neither be foolish – why should you die before your time?"

– Eccl. 7:17 (NKJV)

It is possible that being in the wrong place, with the wrong people, at the wrong time, can cause premature death. At times, a foolish act or decision may bring about an early departure from this life.

I have also known of men and women who continually struggled with some type of drug addiction. They would be free, then bound, free again, then find themselves returning to their addiction, living in a repetitive cycle of up and down—free and bound. At times, they would experience brief seasons of total freedom, making a solid attempt to serve the Lord. Then, without any warning, they suddenly pass away. In some cases, their family knew that they were in right standing with God before they departed, bringing them great comfort. One man who experienced this situation with a member of his family said, "Perhaps God, in His mercy, took them to heaven to prevent them in the future from returning to a life of sin, eventually dying in that sinful condition."

This thought is implied in Isaiah 57:1 (NKJV):

"The righteous perishes, and no man lays it to heart: and merciful men are taken away, none considering that the righteous is taken away from the evil to come."

Years ago, a precious, well-known minister experienced the sorrow of his youngest son being killed in a head-on collision. After many years of questioning "why," Isaiah 57:1 was quickened to him by the Holy Spirit. At the time of the tragedy, his son was a teenager and was serving the Lord. Had he lived longer, he could have turned from Christ. Thus, he was taken to avoid the "evil to come." This certainly is not the case in every situation but may apply in some instances. Jesus noted that it would be better to enter into life (accept Him as savior) lame or maimed than to have all of your body intact and go to hell (Matt. 18:8-9). Jeremiah made this statement:

"Give glory to the LORD your God, before he cause darkness, and before your feet stumble upon the dark mountains, and, while ye look for light, he turn it into the shadow of death, and make it gross darkness."

— JEREMIAH 13:16

I once preached a message on this passage and called it, "Get Me Home Before Dark." In the mind of the heavenly Father, it may be best for an individual to be taken to heaven before some spiritual or moral darkness overtakes them.

Many years ago, at a church youth camp, one of the young boy campers drowned in a swimming pool. He was pronounced dead at the pool by a noted Hindu doctor from the area. My mentor, Floyd Lawhon, was at the pool and began earnestly praying that God would be merciful and raise the lad up. Within minutes, the child began vomiting water and was taken to the hospital where he survived without any complications. However, when he grew older, he was continually in trouble with drugs and in and out of prison. He has spent much of his life behind bars. At one point, his Christian mother said, "At times, I wonder if it would have been better for him to have gone to be with the Lord when he drowned than to live and struggle all his life with drugs, alcohol, and prison."

At times, to avoid any future evil days or to prevent someone from stumbling into the dark (being dominated by spiritual darkness), the Lord permits a person to depart this life, sparing them from an eternity without Him. This is certainly not every case but must be considered with some.

HOW OLD WILL CHILDREN LOOK IN HEAVEN?

There have been numerous stories related by men, women, and children, all who were pronounced clinically dead through an accident or a heart attack. Their soul and spirit returned to their bodies, and they lived to tell amazing stories of life beyond this life. I have personally interviewed individuals of all ages and have read numerous accounts from books and documentaries. Strangely, much of what they describe is similar, with the exception of some minute details that differ depending upon each situation.

Perhaps the most intriguing question asked is when infants pass, will they immediately become a certain age in heaven? Or, if a child passes, let's say from the age of 5 to 12, will they remain the same age in heaven? What about a person who is in their teens? Will they remain the same age, or will they appear older when we see them again?

We know that the aging process ceases once we pass from this earthly life. In the ten generations before Noah's flood, men lived much longer, averaging between six hundred and nine hundred years. The oldest man, Methuselah, lived to be nine hundred sixty-nine years of age (see Genesis 5). Today, the average person lives for 77.5 years. Some never reach this age marker, and others extend far beyond this average lifespan. There are numerous theories as to why pre-flood mankind lived longer. Limited print space prevents me from further exploring possible reasons for these longer lives.

Many studies have been conducted where hundreds of individuals, all who had near-death experiences, were interviewed. They experienced an "out of the body encounter," seeing friends or family members who previously departed this life, some many years ago. I do know that in every life-after-death or near-death experience that I have ever studied, if a person dies at an older age, when a family member sees their spirit in heaven in a vision, dream, or during a near-death encounter, they always appear younger than when they died. Most are described appearing as they did on earth in their late twenties or early thirties. The following story may give us a clue as to why this is the case.

Years ago, I was preaching in Indiana. After a Saturday morning service, the host pastor, Vonda Bishop, asked me to speak with a man whose wife had recently passed away with cancer. She passed when she was in her forties. He told me about his wife's illness and how her death left him to raise several wonderful children. His oldest daughter was seriously grieving her mother's death, causing her father great concern.

One night, a very strange and marvelous event occurred. The daughter was awakened from her sleep by her beautiful mother standing beside her bed. The mother expressed her happiness being in heaven, free from sickness. She revealed how beautiful and wonderful things were.

The daughter expressed to her mom how beautiful she looked. The mother informed her that when you die, angels arrive to carry your spirit and soul from your body to a heavenly paradise. Before entering your eternal abode, the angel asks you, 'How old would you like to look?' She recalled that her favorite age was when she was thirty-one. At that moment, she actually appeared the way she did when she was thirty-one.

After the experience ended, the daughter ran to her father's room to tell him what had happened. When the dad told his wife's closest friend, she began to cry. She said, "When she was dying with cancer, there was a picture in her room. She looked at it and said that it was the best she ever looked, and she was thirty-one. She hoped that when she got to heaven, she would look just like she did in the picture!" I believe this was a revelation from eternity and explains why in heaven, some look younger and some more mature.

I once asked my wife Pam how old she wanted me to look in heaven. She said she thought I was good looking throughout my life, so it didn't matter. If she was seeking brownie points, she hit a home run!

WHY CHILDREN STILL LOOK LIKE CHILDREN

On the other spectrum, what about young children? Often, in the same type of life-after-death or near-death experience, a child who has passed will look the same age, or close to the same age as they did when they departed this life.

Theo Carter was a powerful minister from Kentucky who lived to be in his nineties. In 1947, his nine-year-old son, Charles Edward Carter, was playing in the street shooting off fireworks. He was struck by a truck that instantly killed him. Forty-three years later, in 1990, his wife Thelma was taken to Louisville, Kentucky, for heart surgery. Thelma suddenly died during the surgery. She had been declared dead for twenty-one minutes. They covered her with a sheet and were moving her corpse on a gurney to the morgue to prepare her body. As she was being wheeled to the morgue, she suddenly revived to the shock of the doctors.

Thelma later told her husband that she had died and was taken to heaven. Not only did she see many of the saints they knew who had passed throughout the years, but she also saw their nine-year-old son who had died forty years prior! He knew who she was, calling her Mom. She asked him what he does. He said he played with all of the other children. They even played together on streets that were made of gold. Thelma saw a minister she knew that had passed away many years before her surgery, standing with her son. Charles told his mom, "He is my guardian in heaven. He helps take care of me."

A *child* that can remain the age they were at their death is a marvelous blessing from the Lord. Their parents, siblings, and friends were never able to spend quality time with the infant or child. They didn't get to watch them grow up in this life. In heaven and eternity, they will have the opportunity to enjoy the very one they have missed being with on earth.

YOUR APPEARANCE IN HEAVEN

There are other instances in which a person may look a bit older than their twenties or thirties. When John saw Christ in his Apocalyptic vision, Christ had white hair (Rev. 1:14). This may explain why, after His resurrection, Mary did not recognize His appearance and thought He was a gardener since the tomb was in a garden (John 20:15). The physical shock, the beatings, and crucifixion to Christ may have changed His hair color from dark to white. Christ ascended to heaven in a body that was around thirty-three to thirty-four years of age. I know of very few individuals with solid white hair at that age. We think only of older men and women as being "gray-headed."

The Almighty is called the Ancient of Days, whose garment was white as snow, and the hair of His head was like pure wool (Dan. 7:9). Proverbs 20:29 teaches that "the glory of young men is their strength:

and the beauty of old men is the gray head." The point here is not the color of the hair but the fact that we will have hair. For me, this is an additional plus!

Older adults can look back and remember their lives. They can remember every stage from childhood to high school to adulthood. No one I know would want to look eighty or ninety in heaven if they have an opportunity to look much younger. A child that was never a teenager or adult would have no frame of reference to know how they looked or felt as an adult. It appears that in heaven, children remain as children, for such is the kingdom of heaven.

CHAPTER TWELVE

COMMUNICATING IN HEAVEN WITH THE ANGELS AND THE SAINTS

T he Apostle John was the youngest disciple Christ chose. John outlived the other eleven original disciples by approximately thirty years. In John's day, the Roman Empire ruled and occupied several nations. There were three main languages of which John would have been familiar, Latin, Greek, and Hebrew. The Romans spoke in Latin, the New Testament was written in the Koine Greek (which was also spoken throughout the Roman Empire), and the Jews, especially in Jerusalem, used the Hebrew tongue since the Torah and the prophetic books were penned in the Hebrew language. Hebrew, Greek, and Latin were the three languages written on the inscription above the head of Christ on the cross (John 19:20).

On the Island of Patmos, John heard a voice telling him to "come up here," and he was immediately in the heavenly throne room (Rev. 4:1-2) hearing the voice of "many angels," and the "twenty-four elders" speaking, singing, and worshipping around God's throne. John informed his readers that the four "living creatures" continually cry out, "Holy. Holy, Holy is the Lord" (Rev. 4:7-8).

John heard different voices in this vision. He obviously heard the angels and multitude of worshippers speaking in a language that he *understood*. John wrote that he also heard a multitude from every nation. He wrote:

> "Then I looked, and I heard the voice of many angels around the throne, the living creatures, and the elders; and the number of them was ten thousand times ten thousand, and thousands of thousands, saying with a loud voice: "Worthy is the Lamb who was slain, to receive power and riches and wisdom, and strength and honor and glory and blessing!" And every creature which is in heaven and on the earth and under the earth and such as are in the sea, and all that are in them, I heard saying…"
>
> — Revelation 5:11-13 NKJV

There are two types of languages: *earthly* and *heavenly*. Paul referred to heavenly languages when he alluded to believers who "speak with other tongues" (a supernatural gift from the Holy Spirit), and how it was possible to "speak with the tongue of men and of angels" (1 Cor. 13:1). From the creation of Adam (Gen. 1:27), until the time of the destruction of the Tower of Babel (Gen. 11:7-8), is a period of approximately 2,246 years. Both before and shortly after Noah's universal flood, all men spoke one language (Gen. 11:1, 6). Without going into a lengthy discourse on ancient Semitic languages and the origin of the alphabet, we know that some form of communication existed in both verbal and written forms from the very beginning.

God created the animal kingdom, and we read in Genesis 2:20 that "Adam named the animals." Moses records that the Lord would walk in the garden of Eden, and His *voice* could be heard in the "cool of the day" (Gen. 3:8). According to the Jewish historian, Flavius Josephus, God warned Adam that the world would be destroyed twice," first by water and the second time by fire." Josephus wrote this so that this prediction would be passed on and not be destroyed during these judgments. The sons of Seth wrote the prophecy on stone and on brick in case one was destroyed by the floodwaters, the other would survive. Josephus noted that the pillar of brick erected by them remained in the land of Siriad in his day (Josephus; Antiquities of the Jews, 1.2.3.).

This historical reference indicates that there was an early form of verbal communication and a form of writing used from Adam to Noah, in the first ten generations. There are numerous older scholars that believed the original holy tongue spoken from the time of Adam to the Tower of Babel was some form of what we know as the Hebrew language. Saul of Tarsus, a highly educated Pharisee, could speak numerous languages. However, in his conversion testimony, he states the Lord spoke to him out of heaven "in the Hebrew tongue" (Acts 26:14).

In heaven, there are men, women, and children from all nations and ethnic groups. Most people only speak one language, known as a native language. A native language is the tongue of a particular tribe or people group. Americans speak English, Russians speak Russian, Chinese people speak Chinese, and Hispanics speak some form of Spanish. With so many different languages, how will we all communicate with one another in heaven?

Numerous men and women who have experienced a "life-after-death" or a "near-death" experience often tell of an amazing ability to communicate in heaven through *thoughts, and not words.* It is as though each person can read the other person's thoughts, can ask a question, and have it answered without any verbal communication. This is a common thread in many of the experiences.

During Christ's earthly ministry, when people sat nearby, He could perceive their thoughts (Matt. 9:4). We also read where He "perceived their thoughts" (Luke 5:22), and "He knew their thoughts" (Luke 6:8).

This was not a form of mental telepathy or psychic power but a gift of the Holy Spirit that is linked with the "discerning of spirits" (1 Cor. 12:10). Concerning God, we read that "the Lord knows the thoughts of the wise..." (1 Cor. 3:20), and the Word of God is able to "discern the thoughts and the intents of the heart" (Heb. 4:12). Thought transfers are not impossible because thought patterns can be monitored through electronic equipment.

The entire human body operates through electromagnetic energy. When a patient is in a coma, wires are hooked up to measure their heartbeat, their brain waves, and numerous other electrical signals allowing the doctors to know the "activity" occurring in their brain or heart.

While it is difficult to explain in human-scientific terms, the brain and the heart both have an electrical field that is measurable. Scientists are now developing devices that will one day be placed in airport security checkpoints, that can *read the thoughts* of the mind, and as far-fetched as it seems, early research indicates the possibility of seeing actual images in the brain transmitted in some picture form on a screen. It has been proven that our thoughts and feelings have a measurable electromagnetic reality. Scientists are now indicating that the heart of a person has its own magnetic field that can be picked up by other individuals standing a few feet from another person. This could be why a woman sometimes says, "there is something about that person that just doesn't *feel* right."

The entire spirit world has some form of energy that, when present, can be felt. When an angel is in our presence, there is a positive and very warm feeling that a person can sense surrounding them. However, if evil or unclean spirits are active within a certain space near a believer, there is a very negative, rather cold and frightening atmosphere (some call it an 'energy') that overshadows the area. The presence of the Holy Spirit creates an atmosphere called "the Divine Presence" or the

"Anointing." Those who first experience God's tangible presence say that it feels like "electricity" is flowing over their body.

The human soul and spirit are the center of a person where all life-information is stored. It can be retrieved even when the "person" is outside of their physical body. When Christ died, His body, which held His brain, heart, ears, mouth, and tongue, the organs that house the five senses, was wrapped in a linen cloth and buried in a limestone tomb covered by a two-ton rolling stone. Yet, we are told that Christ "preached to the spirits in prison, in the heart of the earth" (Eph. 4:9; 1 Pet. 3:18). For Christ to minister for three days to a multitude of righteous souls (from the Old Testament era), both Christ and those departed souls had to have knowledge of their past lives. Christ preached the new covenant message to them, until the end of the third day, when He arose, releasing them from this underground prison where they had been confined, according to Peter, from the time of the flood of Noah (1 Peter 3:20).

With the global diversity of nations, what single language will we speak in heaven? How will it be possible for all tribes and people to understand the languages of others? Will everyone suddenly speak one common language?

Let us assume that God's intent is to impart one specific language to all who enter the heavenly kingdom. This is certainly possible after reading the amazing linguistic miracle that occurred on the Day of Pentecost (Acts 2:1-4). Those men (and women), gathered in the upper room (about 120 in Acts 1:15), were predominately Galileans (Acts 2:7). The common people would have spoken the Syriac-Aramaic dialect, which Christ also spoke, as noted in the New Testament, where certain words and phrases require an interpretation from this language for the reader (Mark 5:41; 15:34; John 1:38).

When these simple Galileans were filled with the Spirit, they began to speak with other tongues as the Spirit gave them the utterance (Acts

2:4). Acts 2:9-11 lists about sixteen different regions of the world that the Jews traveled from to get to Jerusalem for this Pentecostal festival. The devout Jews "heard" these Galileans speak in their own tongue and called it amazing and a wonderful work of God (Acts 2:11). The theological debate has been, was God changing the language of the disciples to the actual languages of the people from various nations, or were the disciples speaking in one tongue that was universally understood by the multitude? Was this a change in the apostle's *speech*, or was it a change in the people's hearing?

Obviously, based upon the reactions of the multitude, the actual miracle was in the *speaking* of other tongues. Had the miracle been upon the listener only, then some would have doubted, asking, "what does all this mean" (Acts 2:12). Another confirmation can be found in 1 Corinthians 14:22 when Paul wrote, "Tongues are not a sign to them that believe but to them that believe not."

If these Galileans, who could have spoken Aramaic and possibly a little Greek and Hebrew, could suddenly speak in other languages (unknown to them), then at the resurrection and the catching away of the saints, one divine language can be imparted to every person the moment they enter the portals of the heavenly throne room. Languages are a part of the resume of the Holy Spirit, as He inspired the speakers with languages to speak on the Day of Pentecost. In the New Testament, when individuals were "filled with the Spirit," one of the main signs of this baptism was that they "spoke with tongues," or literally, in various languages that those speaking had never studied or heard (Acts 10:46; 19:6).

Listed among the nine gifts of the Holy Spirit are two vocal gifts called "different kinds of tongues" and "interpretation of tongues" (1 Cor. 12:10). The gift of interpretation enables the receiver to actually interpret the meaning of the unknown tongue to the audience in the language of those present. For example, if a person was to speak in

Russian in supernatural tongues, the interpreter would not be a Russian interpreter but a person who, under divine inspiration (the gift), interprets the language and the basic meaning of the message to those present in the congregation. Growing up, I watched this gift frequently operate among the older saints in the church. Often, the interpretation was so powerful that sinners would run to the altars repenting and pouring themselves out to God.

The Holy Spirit will raise the dead in Christ as He did Christ Himself (Rom. 8:11), and with the Holy Spirit being the language giver, He can impart one heavenly tongue to all people.

HEAVEN — THE LANGUAGE AND THE INTERPRETATION

These two vocal spiritual gifts, tongues and interpretation, impact *speaking* and *understanding*. I have known of many older saints with little or no secular or religious education. They received the Holy Spirit and were given numerous earthly languages in which they could pray and interceded. My father, Fred Stone, had a tenth-grade education. However, according to individuals from foreign nations who could understand him, when the Holy Spirit came upon him, he could speak fluent German, Italian, Latin, and Greek, even though he never once took a course on these subjects. Throughout my travels to the Holy Land, there have been times when I would pray "in the Holy Spirit," and an Arab Christian or a Muslim would understand every word I spoke and told me that I was speaking Aramaic or Arabic.

With this type of manifestation occurring on earth among the people of God, should we not think it possible for two things to occur the moment we are caught up to meet the Lord at His return for the church (1 Thess. 4:16-17)? The first being the possibility of receiving an impartation of a heavenly language that we will all communicate in.

Or, we may be imparted with a gift in our hearing, giving us an ability to interpret each language spoken.

God would not have millions of souls filling heaven with no way for them to communicate with one another. Not being able to communicate would hinder our fellowship. Remember, in the beginning, there was only one language given to Adam that was spoken for thousands of years until God divided the nations into seventy different groups (see Gen. 11). The language division was to restrain men from uniting for a universal, evil cause.

One more example helps us in this understanding. In Babylon, there appeared a mysterious handwriting on the wall in which neither the king nor his wise men were able to interpret. King Belshazzar called upon Daniel. In him was the spirit of the Holy God (Dan. 5:11). Daniel stood before the huge wall and began interpreting the words as they were actually a form of weights and measurements that he would have been familiar with. The message to the king was that "God has numbered your kingdom, and you have been weighed in God's balance and found wanting (falling short)." Daniel continued by telling the king, "Your kingdom is to be divided among the Medes and Persians" (Dan. 5:25-28).

The Spirit of the Lord enabled Daniel to correctly interpret four words, "Mene, Mene, Tekel, Upharsin" (Dan. 5:25-28). As Paul informed us, there is also a "language of the angels" (1 Cor. 13:1), and at times, men on earth can tap into the heavenly mysteries and pray in a heavenly language. God has His system established, and there will be no communication barriers in heaven.

Several years ago, one of the missionaries I support was ministering in a foreign country, in a poor area. No one knew the English language, and they had no way of studying the language. In one service, the missionary began praying individually for the people. A young man began to cry out to God in perfect English. He was amazed and assumed the young man must have studied English. However, the pastor from the region informed him that this boy was a very poor young man from the local village. He could not speak English and did not know English. He had received the Baptism in the Holy Spirit, and God had given him the English dialect.

From Adam to the Tower of Babel, men communicated in one tongue. After the destruction of the man-made high tower, both men and language were dispersed throughout the earth. Each people group was given a specific language. Rabbi's teach that there were seventy languages dispersed that day eventually forming seventy different nations.

VOCAL UNITY IN HEAVEN

Revelation 7:9-10 (NKJV) gives us an amazing insight as to the unity among the nations that will occur in heaven:

> "After these things I looked, and behold, a great multitude which no one could number, of all nations, tribes, peoples, and tongues, standing before the throne and before the Lamb, clothed with white robes, with palm branches in their hands, and crying out with a loud voice, saying, 'Salvation belongs to our God who sits on the throne, and to the Lamb!'"

This massive multitude consists of people from "all nations" and "tribes." The word "nations" is self-explanatory. The word "tribes" is still used to represent the various bands, pueblos, and communities of America's first-nations groups. There are 537 federally recognized tribes in the United States alone! There are presently hundreds of various tribes in nations such as Africa. John wrote of seeing "peoples and tongues." This phrase "tongues" refers to the fact that within this multitude, various *languages* are also represented. However, in the Apocalyptic vision, when each nation began waving palm branches, they were all repeating the same praise to Christ, "Salvation belongs to our God who sits on the throne, and to the Lamb!" John heard this heavenly throng united in their worship, and he understood the words they were speaking. This was either because they were speaking the same language, or this was supernatural, similar to the first outpouring of the Spirit in Acts 2:1-4.

On the Day of Pentecost, we see how the Holy Spirit imparted a "new tongue" or language to the disciples and apostles of Christ. This was a "sign, and a wonder" to all the Jewish listeners gathered at the Temple in Jerusalem for the Festival of Pentecost. The Holy Spirit understands all languages and can distribute not only a specific language but the ability to interpret each language. In heaven, it is evident that the human barriers are eradicated as all believers from every epoch and age will have received a resurrected spirit-body that can and will communicate in God's chosen language. The angel Gabriel said it best when informing a virgin named Mary that she would become pregnant without a man. He said, "With God, nothing shall be impossible" (Luke 1:37).

CHAPTER THIRTEEN

DO DEPARTED SAINTS HEAR OUR PRAYERS AND DO THEY PRAY FOR US?

There are many Christians who believe it is possible and even necessary that an exclusive group of saints in heaven can hear their prayers and even help answer them. This is a concept that few ministers address, but there is a necessity for Biblical clarity on the topic.

There is a vast difference in the way prayer was offered in the Old versus New Testament dispensations. Abraham is called the "Father of us all" (Rom. 4:16) and is the father of the faith. When Moses received the divine revelation to construct the wilderness tabernacle, God revealed the need for two altars: one made of brass and the other of gold. The brass altar was used for burning various daily sacrifices. However, the gold altar served one purpose; to burn the holy incense. The Temple Institute in Jerusalem has traced eleven different types of spices that were mixed together to formulate the incense burnt on the gold altar. It was believed that all the words from the prayers of the righteous went directly to this altar, and when the priest burned the incense, the words ascended upward to God, being protected within the "holy smoke" from this gold altar.

The priests burnt incense twice a day, during the morning and the evening prayers. Psalms 141:2 indicates that this incense represented the prayers of the saints. In a non-canonical book, the book of Tobit 6:1-7, incense was burnt to create an atmosphere that would ban the presence of demons and evil spirits. The Jews were not the only religious group that used incense. Practically every religion in and near the east has traditionally tapped into the use of incense during their religious rituals.

In Revelation, John informs us that there is a special golden altar in heaven where incense is burned, and the prayers of the saints (that reach God) are presented before God:

> "Then another angel, having a golden censer, came and stood at the altar. He was given much incense, that he should offer it with the prayers of all the saints upon the golden altar which was before the throne. And the smoke of the incense, with the prayers of the saints, ascended before God from the angel's hand."
>
> – REVELATION 8:3-4 (NKJV)

Prayer has always been a form of communication between God and man. Abraham was called "a friend of God" (Isa. 41:8), and Moses knew God "face to face" (Deut. 34:10). Both terms indicate closeness and intimacy. There is not a set pattern established in the Old Covenant on how to pray, nor is there a specifically held tradition. However, in early times it was common when praying to the Almighty to approach Him using the name of the one who was in covenant with Him, specifically, Abraham. God remembered His promises to Abraham, including making him a great nation. At times, when the nation of Israel was in trouble, an earthly intercessor would remind God of "Abraham,

Isaac, and Jacob." Once, when God was set to destroy Israel and raise up a new nation through Moses, the old prophet reminded God to remember His covenant with Abraham, Isaac, and Jacob (Exod. 32:13). Note that Israel never prayed *directly* to Abraham, Isaac, or Jacob, but prayed to God reminding Him of the covenant He had with these three early patriarchs of the faith.

Throughout the Old Testament, the Lord would reveal a particular characteristic or ability that He performed and would attach a compound name revealing to His people that particular attribute. For example, Yahweh Rapha, meaning "God my healer." Yahweh Shalom means "God my peace," and so forth. All prayer in the Old Testament was addressed directly to God.

When Christ's disciples said, "Teach us how to pray," Jesus taught them to approach God by calling Him, "Our Father who dwells in heaven," also noting the holiness of His name (Luke 11:1-2). However, one of the major changes initiated through Christ was how we approach our Heavenly Father. Jesus told His disciples in John 16:24, "Up to this point, you have asked nothing in my name, but ask, and it shall be done."

Christ understood an important change that was coming in the pattern of prayer under the New Covenant. He knew that following His resurrection, He would ascend to heaven and take His place at the right hand of God, ever making intercession for us. To approach God, mankind now had a "mediator" (a heavenly lawyer), and when we approach the heavenly Father using the name of Jesus Christ, we are provided direct access to God. Christ is referred to seven times as "mediator" (Gal. 3:19-20; 1 Tim. 2:5; Heb. 8:6; 9:15; 12:24). The Greek word mediator comes from the root word *mesos,* and it means "to stand in the middle," a mediator is a "go-between; one who reconciles." God is approached through one mediator and only one, Jesus Christ. We read, "For there is one God, and one mediator between God and men, the man Christ Jesus; Who gave himself a ransom for all, to be testified in due time" (1 Tim. 2:5-6).

Some noted that when the rich man died and realized that he was eternally confined in hell, he petitioned Abraham to send Lazarus back from the dead to warn his five brothers about the existence of hell. Why would those five brothers even listen to Lazarus? Because Lazarus had begged at the rich's man's house and his brothers were familiar with Lazarus. No doubt, these five men knew Lazarus had died, as he was lying at the rich's man's gate when he died, and someone had to bury the body. Also, the rich man said, "They will believe if one comes back from the dead" (to warn them – Luke 16:27-31). In this story, it appears the beggar and the wealthy-lost-sinner-man died about the same time. It is interesting that one, Abraham did not claim to be the person to answer this man's request, and two, God did not send the poor beggar back to earth from the dead. Abraham said to the rich man that they (his five brothers) had Moses and the prophets. This phrase (Moses and the prophets) doesn't allude to Moses being alive on earth. It was a phrase for the Torah — the first five books that Moses penned in the wilderness that every Jew was familiar with, and the prophets alluded to the writings of the prophets on the ancient scrolls that we have today in our Bible. Abraham made a strong point. If they do not believe the inspired Word of God, neither will they believe one that returns from the dead! *Repenting and getting in right standing with God must occur while you are alive and not after you are dead.*

This is the only example of a departed "saint" (Abraham) being asked to send a person back to warn others. This was a *request* and not a *possibility*. In the twenty-seven books of the New Testament, there is no admonition, command, or even an encouragement for those living to pray to the dead. Paul said it this way, "There is one God and one mediator between God and men, the man Jesus Christ" (1 Tim. 2:5), and in Hebrews 12:24 he said, "And to Jesus the mediator of the new covenant, and to the blood of sprinkling, that speaks of better things than that of Abel." The reason that Christ alone is the sole mediator and intercessor for mankind is that He alone, through His death and resurrection, made the final and complete sacrifice for the sins of mankind, defeating death, hell, and the grave, bringing the possibility of eternal life to all who will receive Him as Savior and Lord.

PARADISE AND THE PRAYERS OF THE SAINTS

Paul taught that all believers that have died, including the most righteous and holy men and women who ever lived, their souls and spirits are now with the Lord in heaven, resting in the paradise chamber of the third heaven; the same area Paul viewed when he was "caught up into the third heaven" (2 Cor. 12:1-4). Biblically, the heavenly intercession for our prayers does not occur in the *paradise region* but in the heavenly court, the area of God's throne room (Rev. 4 and 5). When John penned his vision of heaven, he described God as "seated on His throne with the Lamb (Christ) at His right hand." He indicated there were twenty-four elders round about the throne. These twenty-four men would be the twelve sons of Jacob from the first covenant and the twelve Apostles of Christ from the New Covenant (see Rev. 4:1-11).

John revealed that there are twenty-four "golden vials" (or bowls) positioned before these elders, meaning there is one bowl associated with each elder. This is interesting considering there are twenty-four bowls and twenty-four hours in one day. John indicated that these bowls are full of odors (fragrances), which are the prayers of the saints (see Rev. 5:8). In the earthly tabernacle and temple, it was the burning of the incense on the golden altar that sent forth a sweet fragrance as prayers were presented to God twice a day. Note that the elders are *storing the prayers* but are not linked with *answering any prayers.* The reason for storing prayers is that eventually, the words will "come up before God as a memorial," and the petitions and requests will be answered (see Acts 10:1-4).

In Revelation, John, in his heavenly vision, observed the souls of the martyrs who were killed on earth, as they were "resting" in a massive chamber under the crystal glass-like floor and were asking God, "Oh Lord, how long will you not avenge our blood..." (Rev. 6:10 NKJV). Later, in Revelation 8:3-4, John describes the beautiful golden altar positioned near God's throne in heaven, in which all of the prayers of all of the saints are poured out and mingled with the heavenly incense. When this incense begins burning on the altar, an angel suddenly takes a golden chalice filled with incense, casting it to the earth, releasing judgment on those who slew these righteous individuals. Since Christ makes intercession for us in heaven, this "angel" at the golden altar could be Christ Himself. He is performing the same type of rituals that the High Priest in both Jerusalem temples performed. He is offering incense, which is the prayers of the saints. In context, the martyrs are crying out for vengeance, and Christ is preparing to release His wrath upon the earth.

Throughout the New Testament, there are many admonitions for the saints to pray for one another. However, there is not one indication or Scripture that the saints referred to are the "departed saints," but instead, are strong believers and disciples of the Lord that are still living on earth praying for those who are also living on earth. Some church traditions mark a specific individual as a "saint" after their death. Only if during their lifetime, they met specific qualifications in several distinct elements, including a miracle or several miracles occurring during their life as a result of their prayers. In the New Testament, the word "*saint*" is penned sixty-one times in sixty-one different verses. It is the Greek word *hagios,* and it refers to someone who is spiritually and morally blameless and consecrated to God. The first reference can be found in Matthew 27:52 when the "dead saints" were raised with

Christ at His resurrection. From that moment on, the word "saint" was used for Christ's followers in Jerusalem (Acts 9:13), in Lydda (Acts 9:32), among believers in Corinth (1 Cor. 1:2), also in Ephesus (Eph. 1:1), and in Colossae (Col. 1:2). In all of these references, the "saints" are still living and ministering within local congregations. You will not find one passage where a church or an individual believer was told to approach the throne of God in the name of a departed saint or some very holy person who once lived on earth.

The danger in seeking heavenly intercession from someone outside of Christ is we minimize the *finished work* of Christ and His *High Priestly ministry* of forgiving sins and imparting eternal life. There is absolutely no co-redeemer or second or third intercessor in heaven that represents us. Christ alone is the redeemer, and His ministry is to make intercession for us (Heb. 7:25).

We must remember that the New Covenant that was ratified through the *blood of Jesus Christ* is a legal covenant sealed with Christ's blood. It is not just some spiritual, emotional, or mental ascent where we agree with a verse or two in Scripture. The writer in Hebrew gives a strong argument that before there can be an actual written will read to the living, the person to whom the will belongs must die. Jesus gave us the covenant. He then died, sealing the new covenant after rising from the dead to legally mediate a new relationship between the Father and those who repent and are forgiven.

HEREIN LIES ANOTHER POINT

A true mediator must know the sins a person has committed before they can be forgiven of those sins. For example, if there are thousands of saints that could receive our prayers, they would still not have the *power to forgive our sins*. We are told that Christ is "faithful and just to forgive us of our sins" (1 John 1:9). If it were possible for others in heaven to forgive us, then that "saint" would still be required to present the petition of guilt and innocence in the heavenly court to Christ and the Father. Satan is called the "accuser of the brethren before God day and night." Only one person in the court of heaven is called our mediator, our advocate, and our propitiation, and deals directly with the accuser, and that is Christ (Heb. 12:24; 1 John 2:1; 1 John 2:2).

One man who was very sincere told me he prayed to saints because he believed that Christ was too busy handling thousands of prayer requests. He went to other saints to ensure that his prayer would be received in heaven. When we consider that God knows the number of hairs on our head (Matt. 10:30), every star and calls them all by their names (Psa. 147:4), making Him all-knowing, there is no distraction He encounters that prevents Him from hearing the prayers of millions at once.

There is certainly nothing improper with honoring believers, including spiritual leaders, ministers, and godly saints who have walked with us who are now in the presence of the Lord. However, all these souls are "resting" and have "ceased from their labors," awaiting the resurrection. Heaven's court is directed by God, the judge, Jesus Christ, the Advocate (lawyer) with the witness of the holy angels, and is a nonstop place of activity.

The only New Testament pattern for all prayer is to "ask the Father in Jesus' name" (John 14:13-14; 15:16; 16:23, 26). This is the Biblical and legal method of asking for anything in prayer.

CHAPTER FOURTEEN

ANGELIC ESCORTS AND DEMONIC SOUL COLLECTORS

There are only two ways of spiritually departing this life: dying, having been forgiven, or dying in your sins. Because the human spirit and soul are invisible to the human eyes, when the invisible, eternal spirit is released from the shell of the human body (where it has dwelt), a spirit agent, such as an angel, is required. Angels are also spirits and can see the human spirit. They assist as an escort to a person's final, eternal abode.

There are five facts from Scripture as it relates to this aspect. First, all humans are a three-part being, which consists of one-part flesh, and two-parts spirit; the body (one part), a soul, and a spirit (two parts — 1 Thess. 5:23). The human spirit is invisible to the human eye. This is why it is difficult for some to believe we have an eternal spirit because the spirit cannot be seen. Some are intellectually challenged and cannot accept by faith what they cannot see with their sight. At death, the human soul and spirit must be disconnected and removed from the body. Complete death can only occur when this separation is complete. Ecclesiastes 12:6 speaks of the "silver cord being loosed" at death, and uses certain metaphors to describe the separation of the eternal from the earthly. Once this separation is complete, there are two possible places the soul and spirit will spend eternity. Eternity is a non-stop timeless zone. The righteous in covenant with Christ will spend eternity with the Lord in heaven and later live on the new earth. The unrighteous will be separated from the righteous in the same manner the tare must be separated from the wheat.

As previously discussed, in Luke's story of the rich man and the beggar, the rich man died suddenly (possibly a heart attack) as he seems surprised with his arrival in the land of the lost. We read, "The rich man died, and in hell, he lifted up his eyes." In one moment, he went from closing his eyes on earth to opening his eyes in hell (Luke 16:23). The beggar, Lazarus, on the other hand, may have died of starvation. There is another narrative Christ told involving a rich man recorded in Luke 12.

This following narrative is a parable. In the story, a particular rich man owned property, a home, a family, and was very prosperous. He was a farmer, and his ground had brought forth an abundance, creating a challenge for storage space for his food and grains. He said within himself, "I will pull down my old barns and build greater." His goal was to "eat, drink, and be merry." He commented, "I have laid up for many years." Reaching the peak of his success, this is the part of which he was unaware; the Lord said (Luke 12:20), "Fool, this night shall your soul be required of you. Then whose things will these be?"

In the English translation, the word *required* is used seven times in seven verses. In Luke 12:20, the Greek word is different from the word used in other references and refers to *demanding something back*. In this setting, the man's eternal soul and spirit, which was imparted to the man from God, was being required of the Lord as He was demanding it back through death. This is why Solomon wrote that at death, the body returns to dust, and the "spirit returns to God who gave it" (Eccl. 12:7).

THE ANGELS AND THE SOUL

As previously discussed, the beggar died at the rich man's door. Luke 16:22 says, "And it came to pass that the beggar died and was carried by the angels into Abraham's bosom."

Notice there are angels (meaning at least two) that bore the spirit of this poor man to an eternal resting place. The Greek word *"carried"* means to *"bear up and carry away"* and is also found in Mark 15:1, Revelation 17:3, and 21:10. It refers to being bodily transported from one location to another. In John's reference, he was "carried" in the Spirit to the wilderness to see the harlot riding the beast, and in another reference, he was carried by the Holy Spirit to the New Jerusalem. Angels escort the righteous to their eternal dwelling place in heaven, specifically the third heaven "paradise," where they await the resurrection of the dead. Those who have departed do not have a resurrected body at this moment and will receive their own new body when the Lord returns, at what we term the Rapture. It is clear that in the afterlife, you maintain the same name that you did on earth. On the mount of transfiguration, Moses was known as Moses, and Elijah was still recognized as Elijah. Abraham was called "Father Abraham" by the rich man in hell (Luke 16:23), and the beggar Lazarus was recognized by the same name he used when he begged in a physical body (Luke 16:24).

CHRIST'S ANGELIC ESCORTS

The New Testament presents a dynamic revelation of what occurred between Christ's death on the cross and His resurrection. At three in the afternoon, Christ "commended His spirit" into the hands of His heavenly Father (Luke 23:46). The word *commend* means to present something; the implication is to *deposit something as a trust for protection.* Some scholars teach God took the Spirit of Christ to heaven during the three days His body was concealed in the tomb. However, this is not the case. Paul wrote in Ephesians 4:9 that before Christ ascended back to the Father in heaven, He *"first descended into the lower parts of the earth."* This does not allude to the grave, as the bodies in those days were not buried in the ground. This verse refers to the special compartment under the earth where, for 4,000 years, the souls of the righteous were confined after their death. Christ actually "preached" to these spirits in this underground chamber, and when He rose from the dead, He led these souls out of this netherworld chamber, back to the earth. At some point, they were all taken up to heaven where they reside to this day.

When the disciples arrived at the tomb to look inside to see if Christ's body was actually missing, they encountered two angels. Inside the white limestone tomb, they saw Christ's linen graveclothes, including a folded linen cloth that had covered Christ's face. Inside the tomb, at the top and bottom of the flat stone slab where Christ's body had laid, these angels dressed in white garments proclaimed that Christ was not there, and His disciples should not seek the living among the dead (Luke 24:5). What was the assignment of these angels? I believe it was threefold.

First, the spirit and soul of Christ were to be brought back into His body (the resurrection) that was lying inside the tomb. The tomb was dark, and there was a stone weighing an estimated two tons, blocking access to the tomb's entrance. After Christ's resurrection, He was actually able to walk through a solid door that was shut. I believe Christ *could have* walked through the solid rock stone in front of the tomb's entrance. However, had this occurred, the stone would have remained, concealing the entrance, and the seal placed by the Romans would not have been broken. The tomb could have remained guarded by the same Roman guards, despite the fact that the body inside was actually missing. No one could break this seal without facing the penalty of death. An angel, described as a young man (Mark 16:5), was present to roll the stone away from the entrance, allowing Christ to walk out, and also allowing others to look inside.

> "And, behold, there was a great earthquake: for the angel of the Lord descended from heaven, and came and rolled back the stone from the door, and sat upon it."
>
> – MATTHEW 28:2

Second, when a righteous person dies, angels are commissioned to release their soul and spirit from their body. They are tasked with bringing them into the heavenly paradise. It is possible that these angels were the very ones who released Christ's spirit from His body on the cross. After the separation, they brought it to the lower righteous compartment under the earth in the same manner that the angels carried the spirit of Lazarus to Abraham's bosom the moment he died (Luke 16:22). These two angelic beings mentioned in Luke 24:4 could have served as personal escorts bringing the spirit of Christ back into His body.

Third, the angels were active in announcing Christ's conception (Luke 1:26-31), then nine months later, a heavenly host announced Christ's birth in Bethlehem (Luke 2:10-12). At the conclusion of Christ's temptation, and in the garden of Gethsemane, angels ministered to Him. Angels were present at the resurrection. Two men in white (angels) gave the message at Christ's ascension that He would return to earth again (Acts 1), and angels will ride with the "armies of heaven" at Christ's return and gather "His elect from the four winds of heaven" (Rev. 19:14). Angels were sent to make the announcement that Christ had risen! Angels participated in the resurrection of Christ.

In John's resurrection narrative, he describes two angels in the tomb of Christ, one at the head of the slab and one at the feet. In Luke's story of the beggar who died, there were two angels that carried his soul and spirit into the lower paradise under the earth. When Christ died, two angels would have also released His spirit from His body, carrying it to the underground paradise. As stated at the resurrection, these two angels could have also assisted in bringing the spirit of Christ back into His body (John 20:12). David wrote, "You will not leave my soul in hell neither will you allow your holy one to see corruption" (Psa. 16:10; Acts 2:31). In Psalms 91 verses 11-12, we read, "He shall give his angels charge concerning you, and in their hands they will bear you up."

DOORS AND PORTALS

There are entrances to other worlds. These access points can be termed "doors" or "portals." There are several Biblical references to "heaven opening." In the heavenly realm, John was on the Island of Patmos when he wrote, "I saw a door in heaven open and heard a voice saying, come up hither and immediately I was in the Spirit" (Rev. 4:1-2). This Greek word for door means a literal portal or opening. During Christ's water baptism, when He came up out of the water, we read, "...the heavens were opened unto him, and he saw the Spirit of God descending like a dove and lighting upon him" (Matt. 3:16). Christ informed Nathaniel that he would see "heaven open, and angels ascending and descending upon the son of man" (John 1:51).

There is some type of a heavenly portal that, once entered, brings a person from the atmosphere of earth to the third heaven, or vise-versa, within a short period of time.

If there are portals in which spirits travel from heaven to earth and back, there must also be portals that lead from earth's surface to Tartarus (the Greek word for the lowest hell where fallen angels are bound – 2 Pet. 2:4), where lost souls are confined. According to Scripture, the pits that are under the earth have openings. Several Biblical passages indicate that these entrances to the underworld are located in the waters.

"Let not the waterflood overflow me, neither let the deep swallow me up, and let not the pit shut her mouth upon me."

— PSALMS 69:15

"Or who hath shut up the sea with doors."

— JOB 38:8

"Hast thou entered into the springs of the sea? or hast thou walked in the search of the depths."

— JOB 38:16

"Have the gates of death been opened unto thee? or hast thou seen the doors of the shadow of death?"

— JOB 38:17

"Dead things are formed and the inhabitants thereof. Hell is naked before him and destruction (Abaddon) under the waters hath no covering."

— JOB 26:5-6

"They shall go down to the bars of the pit, when our rest together is in the dust."

— JOB 17:16

All of these verses were written hundreds of years prior to the descent of Christ into the heart of the earth (Matt. 12:40). At that time, both the righteous and the unrighteous dead went to a specific and separate underground gathering place. Notice that these locations are under the earth (Num. 16:30), under the mountains (Jonah 2:6), and under the waters (Job. 26:5).

In the Scripture, heaven is always "up," and hell is always "down." Psalms 55:15 speaks of "going down quick into hell," and Ezekiel 31:16 alludes to being "cast down into hell." Ezekiel also warns of nations who "went down into hell" (Ezek. 31:17). Peter told his readers that fallen angels were "cast down into hell" (2 Pet. 2:4). In the wilderness, when Korah, along with two hundred and fifty princes rebelled against Moses, God sent a strange judgment. We read:

> "And the earth opened her mouth, and swallowed them up, and their houses, and all the men that appertained unto Korah, and all their goods. They, and all that appertained to them, went down alive into the pit, and the earth closed upon them: and they perished from among the congregation."
>
> – Numbers 16:32-33

In this passage, the English word "pit" is the Hebrew word *Sheol*, which refers, not to the grave, but to Hades or underground caverns where the unrighteous now dwell. The word "pit" is used 77 times in the English translation and is often translated from the Hebrew word *bowr*, referring to a cistern or a large hole in the ground. In seventeen places, the word used is Sheol. In all of these references, it refers to the land of the departed souls. Repenting while you live is what releases you from the eternal destination of the pit. Isaiah wrote:

> "O Lord, by these things men live, and in all these things is the life of my spirit: so wilt thou recover me, and make me to live. Behold, for peace I had great bitterness: but thou hast in love to my soul delivered it from the pit of corruption: for thou hast cast all my sins behind thy back."
>
> – Isaiah 38:16-17

Is there a way of "proving" that these entrances exist? Several years ago, a man named Ivan Sanderson claimed to have discovered ten locations on the planet, spaced at equal distances, that hold high levels of electromagnetic energy. Some suggest these energy spots are actually portals (vortexes) that lead to locations under the earth. All of the vortexes have a pyramid shape, and the majority of them are either in the sea or in areas where there is water, separated by the space of seventy-two degreed intervals. They include the famous Bermuda Triangle and the Devil's Sea near Guam; two places noted for their strange electromagnetic energy.

Just as the holy city (New Jerusalem) has twelve gates where people arriving from the north, south, east, and west can enter, it is also possible that when a human spirit is removed from the body of a wicked, unrighteous, and unrepentant sinner, their spirit and soul are pulled through one of these vortexes. These vortexes seem to be located at equal distances around the earth. These could be entrances to the underworld of hell.

THE PERSIAN GULF

The Persian Gulf is a large body of water at the end of the Arabian Peninsula in the Arabian Sea. The Tigris and Euphrates Rivers that border Iran and Iraq form one river that empties into the Persian Gulf. The Persian Gulf trench is about ten thousand feet deep. This is the region where four wicked angels, for centuries, have been bound under the waters of the Euphrates River. In Revelation 9:14, John saw into the Great Tribulation when these angels would be released upon the earth, tormenting men for a set time.

When Jonah was thrown overboard into a raging sea, and the great fish swallowed him, most readers are unaware that Jonah actually *drowned in the sea,* and the great fish swallowed him to preserve his body for three days. We read that he prayed "out of the belly of the fish" (Jonah 2:1), meaning he prayed after he was raised back from the dead. The rebellious prophet describes how he was "cast into the deep in the midst of the sea...and the waters compassed about me even to the soul; the depths closed around me and the weeds were wrapped around my head" (Jonah. 2:3-5).

A revealing part of his confession is when he said, "I went down to the bottom of the mountains; the earth with her bars was about me forever; yet you brought my life up from corruption" (Jonah 2:6). The prophet describes his last moments when he said, "When my soul fainted within me, I remembered the Lord." He even said, "Out of the belly of hell I cried, and you heard my voice…" (Jonah 2:2, 7 NKJV). His rebellion against God led to his death by drowning, and in the underworld, his soul and spirit cried out to God, and in God's mercy, he brought Jonah's spirit back from hell into his body, which had been preserved for three days within the whale.

The internal evidence within the story is clear; Jonah rebelled, was cast overboard, and drowned. As his spirit came out of his body, his spirit and soul saw the "bottoms of the mountains" and the "bars" of the underworld. This is why Christ compared His three days and nights in the heart of the earth with Jonah (Matt. 12:40).

Job had some interesting insight when he wrote:

> "Dead things are formed from under the waters, and the inhabitants thereof. Hell is naked before him, and destruction hath no covering."
>
> – JOB 26:5-6

The word "dead" here in Hebrew is *rephaim*, a Hebrew word used to describe a giant race of men that once roamed the earth. The surface of the earth is one-third land and two-thirds water.

There are various types of spirits that are presently confined in different levels or chambers under the crust of the earth. Some, identified as fallen angels, are now concealed in "chains of darkness," awaiting the future Great White Throne judgment (2 Pet. 2:4). This is why death and hell will "give up their dead," which includes the souls of all sinners, as they will be judged at this judgment (Rev. 20:11).

In 1 Samuel 28:13, a witch who lived in a town called Endor informed King Saul that she saw gods ascending out of the earth." These were familiar spirits of some type who had access to the earth and to the regions of the underworld. This is evident when Satan spoke to God about Job. God asked Satan where he had been, and twice, he answered the same. In Job 1:7, Satan replied, "from to and fro in the earth and walking up and down in it." On a second occasion, when asked where he had been, Satan's reply was the same, "to and fro in the earth and walking up and down in it" (Job 2:2).

The word *walking* is used twice. The first time it is used (Job 1:7), the Hebrew word means to walk. The second time it is used (Job 2:2), the Hebrew word means "to walk all around." The first word, "walk" would imply to walk around in curiosity. Satan was attempting to get into Job's life and onto his property, but a hedge was preventing him. In the second narrative, the hedge had been removed, and he was "walking all around," actually doing as much damage as possible to Job. Satan is not presently in hell as some preach, but is now the "prince of the power of the air" (Eph. 2:2) and the "god of this world" (2 Cor. 4:4). He does, however, have access to both the surface of the earth where people are and the underworld where fallen angels and the spirits of unrighteous men are imprisoned.

A NATURAL AND A SPIRITUAL BODY

In 1 Corinthians 15, the Apostle Paul gives a brief discourse on the resurrection of the dead. He notes that this resurrection process is a "mystery." Those who are the "dead in Christ," meaning those who have died and whose spirits are with the Lord in paradise, will be raised and receive a new "spiritual body." In 1 Corinthians 15:44, Paul writes, "It is sown in a natural body and raised a spiritual body." The natural body refers to the physical body God gave a person when they entered the world. These bodies grew, matured, aged, and will eventually return to the dust of the earth. The spiritual body refers to the type of body the righteous receives at the resurrection.

The word "natural" (1 Cor. 15:44) in Greek, is the word the Greeks used when referring to the soul of a man. The word "spiritual" is from a word used to describe the spirit dwelling within a man (both male and female). Remember that a human is a tri-part being, consisting of a body, one soul, and one spirit.

The physical body is kept alive by the blood, as the "life of the flesh is in the blood" (Lev. 17:11). The soul nature is also linked with the "breath of God," as indicated when God breathed into man's nostrils the "breath of life and man became a living soul" (Gen. 2:7). The soul is linked with the five human senses, hearing, seeing, smelling, tasting, and touching. It is through these five senses that a person connects to the physical world of things they can see, touch, taste, smell, or hear. The world around them becomes their source of knowledge and information. The human soul holds the conscience and the ability to choose between good and evil. The human spirit is different in that the inner spirit is God-conscious. When a sinner encounters the convicting power of the Holy Spirit, the Spirit of God is appealing not just to the intellect but to the spirit of that person, awakening their spiritual conscience, which has been made dead by sin but can be quickened by the Holy Spirit.

The body, while on earth, is a "natural body," and the soulish man is connected with the body. If the person has received a redemptive covenant and repented of sin, then the Spirit that raised Christ from the dead will dwell in them (Rom. 8:11). While a believer lives on earth in a natural body, their redeemed spirit is teaching them how to walk "in the spirit" or follow the spiritual things of God, which prevents the flesh nature from ruling over them (Gal. 5:16).

THE SPIRITUAL BODY

At the resurrection, when Christ returns, a believer will be given a new spiritual body. This does not imply that a spirit body is some form of a floating energy, a fog, or a vaporish life substance without a bodily shape. A spirit body is a body without physical limitations. This body will look similar to the same physical body one has on earth, as far as the facial appearance. I believe this is what Paul alluded to when he wrote:

> "For now we see through a glass, darkly; but then face to face: now I know in part; but then shall I know even as also I am known."
>
> – 1 CORINTHIANS 13:12

One prime example is Moses. This prophet lived one hundred twenty years then died. God buried him in the plains of Moab, concealing his grave to prevent the Israelites from finding it and building a monument to the prophet (see Deut. 34:5-6). It was 1,500 years later that Moses appeared on the Mountain where Christ was transfigured and spoke with Him concerning His coming death in Jerusalem. Peter, James, and John were present, also seeing Moses and Elijah. Moses had not been raised from the dead, yet his spirit was speaking to Christ about the future (Matt. 17:1-3). Christ later called this a "vision," making some suggest that these two men were only apparitions and not literal. This cannot be true. The meaning of the word "vision" is to gaze upon something, a visible spectacle. When Daniel saw a literal angel of the Lord bringing him a message, he called it a "vision" (Dan. 8:26; 9:21) and noted that the men with him saw nothing but began shaking and ran away (Dan. 10:7-8). A vision is not some figment of the imagination but is literal. The point is, Moses literally appeared as did Elijah.

After fifteen hundred years, the body of Moses had long deteriorated in the grave, and according to Scripture, Moses' eternal spirit was speaking with Christ. This would require Moses' spirit to be temporarily brought out of Abraham's bosom, taken to earth, and afterward returned to his underworld abode.

A BODILY OR SPIRITUAL RESURRECTION

There are two theories as to what will make up the resurrected body. Some teach the resurrected body will have flesh and bone and be absent of blood, similar to Christ after He was raised. Others suggest that the resurrected person will have a bodily form that will have the shape and features of a physical body but consist only of spirit-matter and will not be linked at all with the physical world. One may argue that a physical-type body would degenerate again and age as it did in the previous life. However, Christ has a body of flesh and bone and remains in that same form from the moment of His resurrection to the present. If the resurrection occurred in AD 33 (a general date), and John wrote the Apocalypse in AD 95, then there is a 62-year gap. Yet, John saw Christ dressed in a white garment, having brass colored feet, white hair, and fiery eyes (Rev. 1:13-15).

Adam was a flesh man housing a soul and a spirit. He physically lived to be 930 years of age (Gen. 5:5). The oldest man to live was Methuselah, who passed at 969 years of age (Gen. 5:27). The secret to Adam's long life was the tree of life. This tree is now in heaven, and it produces twelve different types of fruit each month. In the Garden of Eden, this fruit sustained Adam and Eve, renewed their bodies, and as long as this first couple ate from the tree, they could have lived in a continually rejuvenated condition (Gen. 2:9; Rev. 22:2).

The mysterious substances of life concealed in the fruit assisted the cells of the body, skin, and organs in revitalizing. After Adam and Eve sinned, God knew that if the couple gained access to eat of the tree of life, they would "live forever" (Gen. 3:22).

Many people view death as a physical event in which the heartbeat ceases, breathing stops, the body becomes rigid, and if you believe the Bible, the soul and spirit exit from its bodily shell. Death, in the Bible, is not just a one-time event, but death itself is an actual spirit. The New Testament gives names to specific spirits, including a spirit of *fear* (2 Tim. 1:7), a spirit of *infirmity* (Luke 13:11), a *tormenting* spirit (1 John 4:18), and a *lying* spirit (1 Kings 22:23).

The proof that death is an actual spirit is found in the Apocalypse. Revelation 6:8 tells of John seeing the famous four horsemen. It is this spirit of death that controls the power of hell:

> "And I looked, and behold a pale horse: and his name that sat on him was Death, and Hell followed with him. And power was given unto them over the fourth part of the earth, to kill with sword, and with hunger, and with death, and with the beasts of the earth."

Death rides a "pale" horse. The word *pale* in the Greek is *chloros* and actually means "greenish." This angel was called "the destroyer" when it passed through Egypt, taking the lives of every firstborn. The Egyptian sons were not protected because the lamb's blood was not on their doorposts as it was on the doorposts of the Hebrew families. Death is considered an "enemy of God" and is the "last enemy to be destroyed" (1 Cor. 15:25-26). John previewed the final sentence God places on death, when in the end, "Death and hell are cast into the Lake of Fire" (Rev. 20:14).

THE DEMONIC SOUL COLLECTOR

With angelic messengers being involved in the collection of human souls and spirits, transporting them into the realms of the just and righteous, what is the end for those who have not obeyed the gospel or die in a spiritually lost condition?

In Christ's narrative of the rich man and the poor beggar, both died at the same time. Angels carried one of them. However, the sinful rich man simply died in one moment and opened his eyes in hell the next. There is no mention of a spirit-being transferring the man from the earthly realm to the underworld, the dark chambers of lost souls. However, it is possible that certain types of spirits might be involved in the separation process of the sinner's soul and spirit.

According to both Testaments, there is such a thing as demonic possession. In the four gospels, Christ's ministry included deliverance and exorcisms from foul, evil, and unclean spirits. In the New Testament English translation, this exorcism is called "casting out devils" (Luke 9:49). If these evil spirits are not removed from a living person, do they play a role in removing the eternal spirit at death from the departed, taking them into an underground region, separating them from God? I often wondered if the witch at Endor was actually seeing familiar spirits take lost souls into the underworld when it said she saw "gods" (spirits) coming up from the ground.

Years ago, my sister Diana interviewed a man named Ronnie Posey, who had multiple near-death experiences involving the third heaven that occurred during an extended coma. While in a hospital, at one point, Ronnie actually died, and an angelic messenger was sent to him, assigned to escort him out of his body, to heaven. Once outside of his body, he and the angel passed by a room that was next to his. The angel showed him a man who had been in a bad car accident while he was driving drunk. Several demonic-looking sprits were near him to carry his soul and spirit to hell. The man began screaming in fear, as apparently, he saw these spirits, and others (medical workers) could not.

Eventually, Ronnie came out of the coma. When he was able to communicate, he told his wife about the strange and frightful incident, involving a man in a car wreck who died. To her amazement, she confirmed to him that a man was brought in that had been drinking, was in a wreck, and he did, in fact, die shortly after they brought him into the very room Ronnie saw.

THE WOMAN WHO DIED WITHOUT REPENTING

In sharing this true story, I must tell you that I have been asked to keep private the name of the person, and their place of employment for the protection of their job.

Years ago, I, along with several others, was in meeting with a businessman. His company cares for men and women who are in their final months of life-threatening sickness, including some that are a few days from death. I met with one of the directors and discovered that she was a strong Christian. Realizing she had witnessed many people die, I asked her two questions. First, did she ever see people pass that she knew were ready to meet the Lord, and had she ever seen anyone die who she knew went to hell?

She confirmed she had personally witnessed both. According to her first-hand accounts, if a Christian is in their final moments, and has a clear, mental awareness, they often describe seeing loved ones, who died in the faith, appear in their room or tell them it is time to come "home" with them. She commented, "They die in peace, and the room is, for a moment, filled with a certain 'electricity,' creating an awesome, almost holy atmosphere. She followed up, relating a very troubling and sad story.

She spoke of an older woman that a family brought to the center so the older woman could spend her final days there. The woman's children told the director, "Just let her die here and don't call us when she does. Just cremate her, and we will pay the bill." This request seemed rather cold and strange, coming from her family.

The woman was given a room, and the director told me that she had never encountered a more hateful, angry person in her life. She continually used profanity and would scream at the staff. This director became concerned for the woman's eternal soul, and despite the house rule of not talking religion with the patients (unless they ask), she went in one day, closed the door, and sat with the woman. The moment she mentioned her spiritual condition, the woman began cursing and screaming at her to get out of her room. She said she did not want anything to do with Jesus or religion. The director apologized, dismissed herself, but the burden for the woman's eternal destination continued to trouble her.

Days later, the director made one more attempt to witness to the woman to no avail. She had the same negative reaction. It was a short time later that the woman was in her final moments of life. She began screaming so loud, the nurses and care workers had to move the patients in wheelchairs to a different part of the building. The director stood in the doorway as the dying woman began describing fire at her feet, moving up her legs and was seeing something horrible. Instead of calling on the Lord, she cursed, and finally died when the fire reached her waist. The director said, "I hope I never again have to see another person die in this manner." She never found out why she hated the Christian faith and despised the idea of serving Christ. Apparently, the family wanted nothing to do with her, as her hate had eaten deep into her soul and spirit.

Testimonies of thousands of near-death moments indicate that a few seconds prior to death, many people who are drug-induced or in a

semi-coma condition, suddenly open their eyes and have a keen awareness of not just their surroundings and the family in the room, but
their eyes are opened into another realm that their family members in
the room do not see. Some doctors suggest this is a chemical reaction
within the body. Others believe it is the soul and spirit being alerted to
their soon departure from this life.

If this were true, and it was merely a chemical reaction, then
every person who is even slightly alert should see the same thing or
see something at death and this does not happen. My granddad, John
Bava, weeks before he passed, called me and said he saw both of his
parents and his little brother who had died in the 1930s on a large
mountain calling him "home." My own father, Fred Stone, told me of
seeing his own father, William Stone, appear at one side of his chair on
several occasions. It happened again just before he passed, nothing was
said, he just looked at my dad and suddenly vanished.

When my dad was dying in a special facility in Cleveland,
Tennessee, he hadn't had anything to eat or drink in about fifteen days,
causing his body to shut down. He had been medicated and was unable
to open his eyes. The entire family was in the room when suddenly, he
opened his eyes wide open and was fully aware of each person. We told
him we loved him, he nodded, then closed his eyes for the final time,
never to open them on earth again. A noted minister in the Church
of God, Ray H. Hughes, also saw his father appear to him prior to
his death. It is difficult to determine if these unique encounters were a
vision or some type of spiritual manifestation.

I believe that prior to the human soul and spirit exiting the body,
there is a moment where the person suddenly perceives (or at times
sees) the invisible veil of the other world and begins to sense their soon
transition from earth to eternity. The reason for seeing departed family
members is that "others" who have previously died are in their soul-
spirit bodies and are already on the other side of the veil. This is often

why a dying person is not aware of the spirit world until the *moment* they are preparing to cross from the earthly to the heavenly, or for others to the netherworld of departed lost souls.

It is clear that the spirit world — in both dimensions, the heavenly and the underworld, are aware of the moment a person is passing, as it is "appointed unto men once to die..." (Heb. 9:27).

CHAPTER FIFTEEN

PREPARATIONS BEFORE THE JOURNEY

With the reality that we have a set appointment with death, the one phrase that would sum up what I would suggest for you to do is, "leave with no regrets, and leave nothing unsaid or undone." It was said of Joshua, "He left nothing undone of what the Lord commanded" (Josh. 11:15). When Isaiah approached King Hezekiah, informing him that his death was imminent, Isaiah instructed the king to set his house in order (Isa. 38:1). The following are four points of wise instruction that a person should make before their final journey.

1. SET THINGS IN ORDER WITH PEOPLE

When Christ understood that His hour had come (John 17:1), He focused His attention to the place where He would die, as we read, "And it came to pass, when the time was come that he should be received up, he steadfastly set his face to go to Jerusalem" (Luke 9:51). To "set your face" means to be determined without wavering, or in Christ's case, to head toward Jerusalem where He would suffer. Moments prior to His death, Christ was setting things in order, as He instructed John to take Mary, His mother, and care for Her (John 19:25-27). Church historians report that the Apostles began leaving Jerusalem between 37 to

44 AD. John took Mary under his care, eventually settling with her in Ephesus, where John resided for twenty-seven years. Mary passed away in Ephesus in 67 AD. John later guided the early churches after Paul's death in 68 AD, until his own natural death in about 100 AD.

Christ made certain that His precious mother would be cared for prior to His death. He knew He would ascend to heaven forty days after His resurrection (Acts 1:3). Before you depart this life, the first step in making preparations is to ensure the ones you're leaving behind are taken care of. This starts with your companion and children. It is also important that the ones left behind to carry on your ministry, business, or other personal matters are given a plan.

2. SETTLE UNRESOLVED ISSUES WITH OTHERS

I know of countless stories where, in a hospital, an older mother or father continued to languish or linger beyond their expected time, because there was someone in their family they desired to hear from, often with an unresolved family situation. At times, it may not be an issue but a desire to see or hear the voice of a person, one more time. In 1998, my grandfather, John Bava, went into surgery. After surgery, he experienced three strokes to the brain, making him unable to move, speak, or open his eyes. However, he could still hear. The doctor said, "He is waiting for someone and will not pass until he hears from them." At the time, I was in Africa and left an outdoor evangelism outreach in Zambia, to fly home. When we got home, Pam and I immediately secured a small plane and flew to Elkins, West Virginia. I spoke to him, sang, and played music on a tape recorder for him. I noticed his heart monitor numbers doubled and tripled, indicating there was internal activity, although his physical body could not respond. He passed two days later.

You must resolve issues with people. Forgive anyone who was abusive, hateful, or unkind to you. If the person dying was wicked in their life or if they were negative and mistreated you, they often feel a sense of remorse but find it hard to discuss. The offended person must tell them they are forgiven. The person will then be released and can die in peace instead of great sorrow.

In Paul's final epistle, before being beheaded in Rome, he mentions several people that had caused him difficulty during his ministry that he was not able to speak to in person. He alluded to Demas, who was once his fellow worker but had departed from the ministry because he loved the world more than Christ. This was a great sorrow to Paul (2 Tim. 4:10). He then mentions an evil coppersmith that did him evil and prayed, "the Lord reward the man according to his works" (2 Tim. 4:14). When Paul was falsely charged with setting Rome on fire, he sadly said, "All men have forsaken me." Yet he wrote, saying, "I pray it will not be held to their charge" (2 Tim. 4:16). He concluded his final letter requesting that someone greet his close, faithful friends for him.

According to his last epistle before he was beheaded, the final parts of Paul's pre-journey preparations were:

- To express his disappointments (with Demas)

- To warn Timothy of enemies that would hinder him

- To forgive those who ignorantly turned against him

- To say a final farewell to all his friends

Earlier in Paul's ministry, a young, inexperienced minister named John Mark, was unable to endure the pressures during a mission trip, causing Paul to send the fellow home in disappointment. The contention was so strong that Paul's fellow companion, Barnabas, left him (Acts 15:39). At the end of Paul's life, he remembered John Mark and asked that he come to see him, as now he was "profitable (helpful) for the ministry" (2 Tim. 4:11). Paul's welcoming of this young man, now mature in ministry, bridged a rift between him, Barnabas, and John Mark.

Setting your house in order includes clearing up any division, confusion, or misunderstanding wherever possible. It is good to pass with a clear conscience toward God and man. Paul wrote, "I exercise myself, to have always a conscience void of offense toward God, and toward man" (Acts 24:16).

A person's conscience is cleared through confessing and asking for forgiveness, or through clearing up misunderstandings in face to face conversations.

3. SET THINGS IN ORDER SPIRITUALLY

When Christ was hanging on the cross, He looked below Him at the men responsible for His painful crucifixion and prayed, *"Father, forgive them for they know not what they do"* (Luke. 23:34). During Stephen's final moments, as men were casting stones at him, he prayed, *"Lay not this sin to their charge"* (Acts 7:60). Paul was willing to forgive others when he wrote, *"I pray it will not be laid to their charge"* (2 Tim. 4:16). The Greek word "charge" in 2 Timothy 4:16, means "to take an inventory, putting something on a list." This refers to the list of deeds an individual performs on earth that is recorded in the books of heaven. Paul is asking God to forgive the person so that their actions will not be on the list at the heavenly judgment.

In John 20:23, Christ gave a powerful revelation on forgiveness, when He said that whosoever sins that we remit, they are remitted to them. We can *choose* to release a person who has sinned against us or offended us.

There have been many individuals whose final moments involved a confession of their sins and repentance. This is often called a "death bed confession," and some people feel uncomfortable with such a late confession. However, the thief on the cross was moments from death when he asked Christ to "remember him" in the future, eternal Kingdom. Christ replied, "Today you shall be with Me in paradise" (Luke 23:42-43). As long as there is breath, it is never too late to cry out for forgiveness. New life is released through repentance.

A dying person must be certain that their "spiritual house," meaning their soul and spirit residing within their body, has been cleansed by the blood of Christ, is forgiven, and their name has been written in heaven. This is the most important aspect of "getting your house in order."

4. SET THINGS IN ORDER FINANCIALLY

In America, seven in ten people die in "testate," meaning without a will. Often, after they pass away, their assets can be tied up in probate with additional financial burdens and costs falling on the surviving family members who have to hire lawyers for court battles. I have observed family members who, on the surface, love each other, until their mom and dad pass, and suddenly, they become enemies over what they did not know was recorded in the will. Trust me. People will fight one another legally if money is involved. They battle over who inherits the house and property, who gets Mom's jewelry, the cars, and access to the checking and saving accounts. Without a legal will, things can become messy and divisive. You should prepare a will, a trust fund, or a revocable or irrevocable trust in advance. The best action to take is when you are *alive and in your sound mind*, to ensure that your desires are carried out beyond the grave. Do not delay this. On the other hand, some give their gifts to their family in their older age while they are still living. Either way, prepare.

5. LEAVE A SPIRITUAL LEGACY

My dad served as a pastor for years, and later, as a traveling minister several years before he passed away. Dad and Mom had a house, two cars, their furniture, clothes, and not much else, including no investments. When he was dying, he said, "Son, I never prepared for this day. I have no money in investments, or anything to leave you kids but some books and a small retirement income from the Church of God that your mother will get for a few years. I regret I have nothing to leave you, kids."

I told him that he was leaving the family with the greatest gift any minister could leave his family. He was leaving me with his good name. His name never had one touch of scandal or confusion connected with it. Fred Stone was a man of God, and everyone who encountered him knew it. He prayed constantly, fasted often, saw countless miracles of healing, and was without moral blemish either personally or in his ministry. He was a simple man who loved rural churches and mountain people.

My family name is important to me because it is also the name that I passed down, and it will continue to be passed down in generations to come. The Stone legacy was built on men who worked hard for what they had. Working in the coal mines of West Virginia, my grandfather, William Henry, would never have guessed the legacy his name would carry today.

The following poem sums up a "spiritual legacy." It was written by a woman named Nelle A. Williams and is titled "Your Family Name." To make it personal, I put my family name as the title and added a few words.

STONE

You got if from your father, it was all he had to give.

So, it's yours to use and cherish, for as long as you may live.

If you lose the watch he gave you, it can always be replaced.

But a dark mark on your name, son, can never be erased.

It was clean the day you took it, and a worthy name to bear.

When he got it from his father, there was no dishonor there.

So, make sure you guard it wisely, and after all is said and done

You'll be glad the name is spotless, when you give it to your son.

Before your final journey, be sure you leave with a clear conscience, your sins forgiven, and good memories. Be memorable to the point that they are still talking about how you are missed, years after your departure.

CHAPTER SIXTEEN

15 DIFFICULT QUESTIONS ANSWERED

I have been asked many questions concerning many Biblical topics in my forty-four years of ministry. Along with prophecy, I often receive questions on heaven and life after death. I have taken fifteen of the most frequently asked questions concerning heaven and answered them.

Question: Jesus spoke of entering into life "halt or maimed" (Matt. 18:8). Does this mean if a person has a physical defect in their limbs, or are unable to walk properly, that they will continue in that physical condition when they enter into eternity at death?

Answer: In the context of the verse alluded to, Christ is warning His adult audience not to offend a small child, as a person doing so would be in great danger, to the point it would be better for them to tie a millstone around their neck and jump into the sea (Matt. 18:5-6). He then expressed the danger of a person being cast into "everlasting fire." Christ said it would be better to "enter into life halt or maimed, rather than having two hands and two feet and being cast into everlasting fire" (Matt. 18:8). The English word "halt" is to be unable to walk. The word "maimed" is an English word whose translation alludes to the loss of a limb, either an arm or a leg.

Entering into life is a phrase that alludes to entering into eternal life, as opposed to being cast into eternal fire. This *does not* imply that a person who was missing a limb or was unable to walk properly on earth will remain in that condition in heaven. The thought here is that it would be far better to suffer or sacrifice now, including whatever it takes to prevent you from sinning, then to allow your feet, hands, and eyes to sin, and then end up eternally lost.

This body of imperfection dies and will eventually return to dust. At the resurrection, a new body is formed without bodily handicaps. One reason some ask this question is that Christ carries the wounds of His suffering after He was resurrected. Christ told Thomas to touch the nail prints in His hands and to thrust his hand into His side, where the Centurion's spear had left an opening (John 20:27). If our wounds are erased, and our resurrected bodies are completely healed with no imperfection, then why is Christ required to eternally carry evidence of His crucifixion?

The answer is judicial evidence. First, when Christ sets up His kingdom, the prophet said people would ask Him about the wounds in His hands (Zech. 13:6), as the Messiah is to have pierced hands and feet (see Psa. 22:16). Christ's wounds will be visible evidence to the Jewish people that Christ is the true and only Messiah. Second, there will be a Great White Throne judgment in heaven, in which all sinners are brought up out of hell to be judged, including Satan and all fallen angels. The scars on Christ are the undeniable proof that He died, initiated a redemptive covenant, and was raised from the dead. The entire event was not a hoax but was all true. The scars will be visual proof at the judgment of who He is. Christ will be the only individual in the eternal kingdom of God that will bear evidence of being wounded on earth as evidence that He alone fulfilled prophecy.

Question: I always heard there would be no tears in heaven, yet we read that God shall wipe away all tears from our eyes (Rev. 21:4). Why is there a need to wipe away tears, and why would anyone be crying in heaven if everything is perfect?

Answer: When the spirit is out of the body, it still retains the same five senses that it had while in the body. Christ stated that if a person ends up in hell, there would be "weeping, wailing, and gnashing of teeth" (Matt. 13:42). The Greek word "weeping" alludes to lamenting, and the root word means to "sob." This is not a metaphor or an allegory, but literal weeping. Individuals will realize where they are and how they are eternally confined, weeping uncontrollably.

Those whose journey ends in heaven will be elated and overjoyed at their arrival. However, at the believer's judgment (the Bema Seat of Christ), all believers will be judged for their words and deeds during their life on earth. John exhorted that followers of Christ would "abide in Him... that we may have confidence and not be ashamed at His coming" (1 John 2:28). Christ told the church at Philadelphia to "hold fast what you have, that no one may take your crown." (Rev. 3:11 NKJV). Paul wrote of the Judgment Seat of Christ, revealing that some individuals will have no eternal reward, as their actions on earth will be tested at the judgment and be burnt by fire, just as wood, hay, and stubble are burned (1 Cor. 3:12, 15).

I have pondered when all tears would be wiped away, and I believe it is linked with this judgment. If we were not as faithful as we could have been, did not work for the kingdom as we should have, allowed someone else to give finances, and we seldom supported ministries in the harvest field to reach the lost, we will be *ashamed* and will not *receive a reward*, as someone else, who did what we should have, will receive our crown. Although we may weep for our lack of working for God on earth, God will still wipe away our tears, allowing us to enter the eternal kingdom. Twice we read that God shall "wipe away all tears from their eyes" (Rev. 7:17; 21:4). This verse will be completely fulfilled, because death, sorrow, and pain, the former things, will have passed away (Rev. 21:4). Once we enter the new heaven and new earth, there will be nothing to cry about!

Question: I am not saying this in any disrespect, but why do ministers make such a big deal about gaining an eternal crown in heaven, or having some type of reward? For me, the "big deal" is making it to heaven and not what we can get as some big reward. Am I wrong?

Answer: God created all human beings, male and female, with a unique, "reward center" in their brain. There are both natural chemicals and neurons that trigger the reward center of the brain. These are designed to personally motive us, in some manner, to work or perform at a higher level. For example, the promise of a pay raise for increased productivity, the possibility of a team winning the championship, the thought of an award for a project, or even honor and recognition for one's work, are all a part of how reward-possibilities motivate people.

Working for the kingdom of God, feeding the poor, clothing the naked, caring for the sick, visiting prisoners, giving water to the thirsty, and winning souls, are examples of these acts of service. The followers who do these things and more are promised an eternal reward. Our work and rewards given by men on earth are temporal, and we leave them when we die. All rewards in heaven are eternal and incorruptible, including a "crown of glory that will never fade away" (1 Pet. 5:4). A crown given to us from the Lord is visible evidence that *we did something* valuable for Him on earth. A person without a crown is evidence of a life wasted that wasn't productive for the Lord. In Revelation 4:10, the twenty-four elders are seen bowing down, laying down their crowns before Christ. If you receive a crown, you will forever have something to lay before Him in thanksgiving. You will also be marked as someone who was faithful and obedient, as a crown is visible proof of that. Thus, rewards are eternally significant for the receiver and for Christ.

Question: Why is it necessary for a new heaven and a new earth to be created in the far future? Why isn't the earth that we now live on, and the heaven that we now see not good enough to continue to exist?

Answer: The phrase, "new heaven and the new earth" is found four times in the Bible (Isa. 65:17; 66:22; 3 Pet. 3:13; Rev. 21:1). Isaiah said, "For behold, I create a new heaven, and a new earth: and the former shall not be remembered, nor come into mind." God created the heavens and earth in ages past (Gen. 1:1). About 1,658 years after Adam, a universal flood covered the planet, destroying all living things with the exception of eight people (including Noah), and the animals on an Ark. This was the first global destruction. In 2 Peter 3, Peter reveals a second total destruction that will again occur, this time by fire:

> "Whereby the world that then was, being overflowed with water, perished: But the heavens and the earth, which are now, by the same word are kept in store, reserved unto fire against the day of judgment and perdition of ungodly men."
>
> – 2 PETER 3:6-7

Christ said, "Heaven and earth shall pass away..." (Matt. 24:35). Peter also stated that the "heavens shall pass away with a great noise, and the elements shall melt with fervent heat, and the earth also and the works that are therein shall be burned up" (2 Pet. 3:10). This burning up of the earth and the creation of a new earth must occur before the holy city (New Jerusalem) comes down from God out of heaven to the earth to tabernacle with men (Rev. 21:2-3). This will occur after the Great White Throne judgment (Rev. 20:11-15). What is burned will be the surface of the earth, which will also consume the seas and oceans. John noted that at that time, "There was no more sea" (Rev. 21:1). This was significant to John, who, when he penned the Apocalypse in about A.D. 95, was a prisoner on an island, surrounded by the waters of the Aegean Sea.

This purging of the planet will likely occur while the Great White Throne judgment is taking place in heaven. All saints from all ages and angels, both good and bad, and all sinners who died and were in hell, will all be present at this judgment. After this judgment, all lost souls (the unsaved), all fallen angels, including Satan, along with death, and hell are cast into the Lake of Fire (see Rev. 20:10-15). Fire purges and purifies, and this global fire will destroy all diseases, plagues, viruses, and the entire earth will be recreated by God Himself, climaxing with the city of God descending to earth, becoming the new headquarters for Christ where He and God will dwell among men. Sin, death, demons, Satan, and all evil will be banished. God said, "I make all things new" (Rev. 21:5). This is what He was referring to. It appears that God is starting all over again, and as things were perfect in the beginning, they shall conclude perfect in the end. This "end" will actually be the beginning!

Question: I have outlived three companions and am now quite old. When each husband died, I loved them very much. Also, when I remarried, I adored the other men that God sent me, and all of them were faithful Christians that went to heaven. When I arrive in heaven, will I feel awkward seeing or being around all three of these men that I knew intimately?

Answer: Christ was once asked a similar but different type of question. In the Torah law, if a husband died and had a brother, he was to marry the widow and bear children so the name of the departed husband would not perish from the earth. The question being posed was if a woman married seven different brothers, all who died without giving the woman a son to carry on her first husband's name, the Sadducees (who didn't believe in the resurrection from the dead) asked Jesus, "at the resurrection, whose wife will she be" (Mark 12:18-23)?

Christ answered that at the resurrection, men and women are neither *married* nor *given in marriage* (Mark 12:25). These two phrases refer to a *contract* marriage or a marriage that is *arranged* by the parents. God provided marriage to prevent man from being "alone" (Gen. 2:18). Marriage is for earthly companionship and for the procreation of families. With the birth of a son, the name of the father continues and expands the human race.

For those who were or are married and greatly love or loved their companion, being with them in heaven is a desire everyone has. However, heaven is so perfect, and the loving atmosphere is so complete that we will be one happy family living in complete peace and joy. A person will recall their relationships in heaven with those who are in heaven with them. There is no indication of any awkwardness or confusion in any manner. In heaven, everyone will be as one family, united for eternity, with former things being past and all things before us new.

Question: I do not understand how there can be a resurrection from the dead when millions of bodies have already returned to dust, and there are no more traces of them on earth. What is there that can be resurrected?

Answer: God told Adam that when he died, his body, which was created from the ground, would return to the dust (Gen. 2:7). At death, the spirit (and soul) of a righteous, born again individual comes out of the body and returns to God. At the coming of the Lord, Paul taught the dead in Christ, meaning those who have died with Him, will come out of paradise with Christ when He returns for the living saints (see 1 Thess. 4:14).

Several scriptures speak of the dust and the resurrection. Daniel wrote, "And many of them that sleep in the dust of the earth shall awake, some to everlasting life, and some to shame and everlasting contempt" (Dan. 12:2). Isaiah described it this way, "Thy dead men shall live, together with my dead body shall they arise. Awake and sing, ye that dwell in dust: for thy dew is as the dew of herbs, and the earth shall cast out the dead." (Isa. 26:19). In both scriptures, the departed have long passed, and over time, their bodies and bones have returned to the dust of the earth.

Paul wrote about the resurrection calling it a "mystery." He taught that a natural body is sown (into the ground) but raises as a spiritual body (1 Cor. 15:44). Paul used an analogy that every seed looks similar, but produces a different plant. All flesh is different, including the flesh of animals (1 Cor. 15:38-39). The bodily resurrection is like a seed. A seed (outer shell) must die in the ground to produce the life that is concealed in the seed. The future plant, a tree, a fruit tree, a grain, is all inside the seed. From the ground comes forth a living plant. This is an amazing, natural phenomenon.

At this time, the spirits of departed souls are in an eternal state, meaning a condition of non-death. However, none who have died "in Christ," now living in the third heaven, have yet received a *glorified* body; that is a transformed body that is tangible and touchable, which is the type of body Christ has since He was raised from the dead. At Christ's return for the church, He will bring the spirits of the righteous with Him and rejoin each spirit with a glorified body. Much of how this is possible, still remains a mystery.

Question: If we have a family member who died in sin and did not make it to paradise, but is separated from God in hell, at the Great White Throne judgment, will we see them among the multitude and will we know they are headed to the Lake of Fire?

Answer: The Great White Throne judgment is where God judges those who lived during the thousand-year reign of Christ (Rev. 20:4), those who died over the centuries, who were confined in hell, and the fallen angels. The saints will certainly be in heaven during this judgment, as, soon thereafter, the earth and heaven will be renovated by fire. It would be a sad and frightening occurrence, if we, as resurrected, glorified believers, saw our loved ones separated from us forever. Isaiah noted that at the time of the new heaven and new earth, the "former things will not be remembered nor come into mind" (Isa. 65:17). Some believe this is when God will erase our memories, specifically of anyone we knew who died lost.

At the time of this judgment, the New Jerusalem will be the home of all of the satins of God who have already been judged at Christ's Judgment Seat (Rev. 11:18), and a home to those who also lived with Christ on earth during His thousand-year reign as the King of Kings. Some suggest that during portions of this judgment, millions of believers and overcomers will have access to the New Jerusalem while this judgment is transpiring.

There is a scripture that contradicts this theory. At some point, either before or after judging people from earth, there will be a set time, with believers present, when God conducts the judgment of the angels. Paul wrote, "we shall judge the angels" (1 Cor. 6:3). Paul wrote these powerful words:

> "Do ye not know that the saints shall judge the world? and if the world shall be judged by you, are ye unworthy to judge the smallest matters?"
>
> – 1 CORINTHIANS 6:2

Judging the world would include being present at this judgment. It is possible that the condemning of these human individuals will be all at once and not on a one-on-one basis, such as at the Judgment Seat of Christ. Those from hell already know their doom is set. Yet, God allows this judgment to show them the *reason* why they are being condemned. It is similar to a judge in a courtroom, setting the punishment for the individuals who have been tried. Also, as far as seeing a single individual, this judgment will be with multiple billions of people at once, which makes it highly unlikely a person would see one individual or a particular family member.

Question: Do the spirits of infants and children go to the same paradise as adults?

Answer: There is not a direct verse that answers this. However, when David's son (with Bathsheba) died seven days after he was born, David made a fascinating statement. He said, "Can I bring him back again? I shall go to him, but he shall not return to me" (2 Sam. 12:23). This statement implies that David would, at his death, see or be rejoined with the spirit of his infant son in the place where departed souls are gathered together. In the Old Testament era, this "paradise" was situated under the earth's crust and was one massive area where the righteous departed souls were gathered for about 4,000 years.

Since paradise is now in the third heaven, it is unclear in the Bible how many various sections or levels exist. For those who die as martyrs, they are commanded to rest in a special area that now exists, situated under the crystal floor that John saw when standing at the golden altar in heaven (see Rev. 6:9-11). These departed souls are all given white robes and told to rest for a little season (Rev. 6:11).

As far as children, there is no specific scripture that reveals either an infant or a child's paradise. However, at various times throughout history, there have been godly individuals who were pronounced dead and have returned to tell amazing stories of their experience in heaven. One such example that was known over one-hundred years ago was a woman who was deathly sick, who passed temporarily and was taken by an angel to an "infant paradise." Each infant spirit is brought up and cared for by an angel of the Lord. Just as a child grows and is taught on earth, each infant is given a personal guardian angel that teaches them about Christ, about heaven, and when they reach a certain age of maturity, they are released into the children's level of heaven. A spirit grows within a human body as the body grows from an infant to an adult. Thus, it is possible the smallest infant spirits grow to a certain size.

Many years ago, while on a fishing trip outside of New Orleans, I was in a hotel. In the early morning hours, I thought I had experienced a sudden heart attack and had died. In a dream-vision, I was taken to paradise and saw several interesting scenes. I actually saw one of Pam's closest friends, Tracy Davis, that had been killed in a car accident in the Birmingham, Alabama, area. She was leading children in songs. What impressed me was this area had beautiful small hills, grass, and trees, including thousands of small houses that had been built for each child. They were all similar, very cute, and resembled the types of houses from the nation they were born to. They were side by side and constructed on small hills. The children were all gathered in the same beautiful area. It had the atmosphere of a huge youth camp. They were having a wonderful time and were being led by adults, who on earth, had loved children's ministry! I sensed that no child was superior in authority, and everyone was treated equally. I also knew there was no lack among them.

Since the kingdom of heaven is made up of children (Matt. 19:14), I am certain that God has these spirits of infants and children well taken care of, and it is likely at this time, children are playing with other children. Once the coming of the Lord has occurred, and the resurrection takes place, all of the saints will live for a few years in heaven and then return to earth during the millennial reign.

Question: I have often heard people say that if God is such a good God, He would never send anyone to hell and that the theology of hell was actually started by the Catholic Church to frighten people into serving God. They say, "I cannot see God sending people into hellfire forever." This would be cruel and unusual punishment. How do you answer this?

Answer: These types of statements have been used as a philosophical form of reasoning to reject the idea of eternal punishment. On earth, if a man has raped and murdered children or young girls, most people with a conscience do not resist the idea of capital punishment or even the death penalty for such crimes. There are also individuals who serve multiple life sentences for criminal activities.

First, we must understand that hell was "prepared for the devil and his angels," as a place to confine these spirit rebels (Matt. 25:41). When men began rebelling against God, and later His covenants, refusing to repent, the same location (hell) became the place where the spirits of rebellious people would also be confined. God, from the beginning, provided various paths that a person could take to be redeemed from eternal damnation (sacrifices, prayers, and repentance). The final sacrifice for our sins was and is Christ. If we confess our sins and believe upon Him as Savior, His redemptive covenant prevents us from entering the eternal world of lost souls.

The part that often disturbs people is the "fire" Jesus alluded to in hell, along with the future "Lake of Fire." The physical body reacts in pain the moment a flame is placed on the flesh due to the sensitivity of the human nervous system. The human spirit and soul operate with five senses but do not have the same nerves the body has. The fire is tormenting, as attested to by the rich man who, in hell, confessed, "I am tormented in this flame" (Luke 16:24). In his case, his tongue was continually burning, perhaps because he never fed a poor man that begged at his gate, while he enjoyed food. The fact that he said "flame," and wanted water for his tongue, could indicate that whatever a person did on earth that prevented them from entering the kingdom of Heaven, could be the part of their spirit that will continually burn and be tormented.

I do not underestimate, nor do I consider the flames in hell as a metaphor. Under this earth, there is fire and heat. However, I believe the worst part of hell will be the feeling of separation from God and separation from the feeling of God's love and peace. It is best for a person to serve the Lord with all of their heart and not take a chance on being separated from the Lord.

Question: When a person is in sin without Christ, and they are about to die perhaps in a sudden accident, most people have one of two opinions: one is that they have time to repent even if it is only a few seconds and the other view is that there is 'no sudden near-death confession' and God wouldn't receive it. This is confusing to me, and which one is it?

Answer: The best example is the thief on the cross. As an evangelist, I often give an altar invitation and invite sinners or backsliders to pray a prayer, sincerely repenting and asking for forgiveness, accepting Christ as their Savior. This altar invitation has been a tradition among the revivalist type meetings for hundreds of years in England and America. The thief on the cross, who was receiving a death penalty for being a robber, was in the final moments of his life when he said, "Lord remember me when you come into your kingdom." Jesus then answered, "Today you shall be with me in paradise" (Luke 23:42-43).

It struck me that this man did not "confess his sins," as he and Christ both already knew he was a sinner (a robber and thief). Neither did this dying criminal go into a long prayer of godly sorrow and deep repentance. The key to his conversion was that he acknowledged and believed who Christ was, as this is the first prerequisite to salvation, "Believe upon the Lord Jesus Christ and you shall be saved" (Acts 16:31). He also acknowledged the "kingdom," which Christ would oversee, and wanted to be remembered in Christ's future kingdom (Luke 23:42). My point is, this could very well be called a "death bed confession," a term used for someone repenting and turning to God moments prior to their death.

The only sin a person cannot be forgiven of is blasphemy against the Holy Spirit (Luke 12:10). Outside of this, Christ forgives all manner of sins. As long as a person has breath and can reason with their mind and heart, they can turn to God in faith, asking for forgiveness and repenting of their iniquities even seconds prior to their death.

One should understand that a sincere death bed repentance can get a person into the kingdom by the "skin of their teeth." However, a person who turns to God at such a late moment will have no reward or crown in heaven, as they spent their entire life in sin and did nothing in the form of good works to gain a reward. It is far better to serve God all of your life than to depend upon a sudden last-minute turning to Him.

Question: I often hear ministers speak about "doing good works," which disturbs me because the Bible teaches that we are saved by faith and not of works. Isn't this dangerous to teach since works have nothing to do with getting into heaven?

Answer: I think you have confused "salvation by works" with "rewards according to your works" (Matt. 16:27), which are two opposite ends of the pole. There is no salvation by fleshly works or through spiritual works. The Bible teaches, "By grace are you saved through faith… it is the gift of God, not of works…" (Eph. 2:8-9). Salvation is through repentance, confession of Christ, and faith in His finished work on the cross. On the other hand, the rewards, including crowns and positions in the kingdom, will be judged according to the works (acts and deeds) we did while living on earth. Matthew 25 mentions feeding the poor, visiting the prisoner, clothing the naked, visiting the sick, and helping strangers among us. Christ even attached a reward to giving a person who was thirsty a glass of cold water (Matt. 10:42). Our treatment of others, our spiritual attitude, our involvement in ministry, and helping others are all attached to the eternal rewards.

The phrase, "good works" is referred to sixteen times in the New Testament. Peter told believers that Gentiles would see the good works of believers and glorify God (1 Pet. 2:12). At the believer's judgment, Paul wrote that our "works" will be tried as by fire. Some, their works will be consumed, but for the faithful, their earthly deeds and actions will stand the test. Those whose earthly works come through the fire will receive rewards. Others will receive nothing (see 1 Cor. 3:12-15). Paul said, "If any man's work shall be burned, he shall suffer loss: but he himself shall be saved; yet so as by fire" (1 Cor. 3:15).

Salvation is a free gift, presented to us on earth, that is received by faith and repentance. Once we are saved, we begin working for the kingdom by helping people and winning souls. The words and deeds are "tried" on the altar of fire at the Bema judgment, and if we have been faithful and true, we are blessed with many rewards (crowns) that are eternal and will never fade away (1 Pet. 1:4; 5:4).

Question: At the judgment, we are informed by Christ that "Every idle word that men shall speak, they shall give an account thereof on the day of judgment" (Matt. 12:36). First, what is an "idle word," and second, how can God record every idle word of every person who has lived?

Answer: As to how God can recall every idle word, that question can be answered this way. There are an estimated 100 sextillion stars in the known universe, yet we read, "He (God) tells the numbers of the stars; He calls them all by their names" (Psa. 147:4). This number, known only to God, is "astronomical." Right now, alone, there are an estimated 8 billion people living on the earth. If you were to calculate the number of people from Adam to this very day, there is no telling the number of people who have lived on earth in humanity's history. The number would be incomprehensible as every second someone is born. Some suggest the number would be as high as 108 billion people! Yet, the Almighty has a book in heaven with the foreknowledge of individuals (Psa. 139:16). The Lamb's Book of Life records the names of the righteous (Rev. 21:27).

One computer in America can record billions of words an hour. We should not think it odd that God knows every word and conversation that has ever been spoken from the beginning of time.

In Christ's statement, the Greek word "idle" is *argos* and can mean lazy and useless. It alludes to being careless with what you say with your mouth. It refers to words with no value; words that do not edify but tear down, criticize, and are hateful and harmful. Giving an *account*, oddly, is the Greek word logos, and is often translated as "word" throughout the New Testament. What Christ is saying is you will be required to give an explanation as to the worthless conversations you've employed!

There is one way in which to clear the account of the negative words you have spoken. Go to the individual or individuals personally, face to face, that you have spoken against or used words to harm or hinder, and ask for their forgiveness. It is better to correct the account on earth than to answer for it at the judgment.

Question: If God would give mankind the opportunity to repent and avoid hell, then why would God not give Satan and the rebellious angels the same opportunity, to repent, change their ways, and spend eternity with God in heaven and on the new earth?

Answer: There are individuals who become so hardened in their mind and spirit that they are "turned over to a reprobate mind" (Rom. 1:28). They are given over to their own lust and evil desires and have *no desire or intent* of ever repenting. As stated in Scripture, there is only one sin, *blasphemy against the Holy Spirit* that cannot be forgiven. The Bible also speaks of people who have sinned to the point that their conscience becomes "seared with a hot iron" (1 Tim. 4:2). This phrase alludes to a conscience that is calloused, hard, and unable to feel normal emotions or conviction.

Satan led a pre-adamic rebellion in heaven, where one-third of God's created heavenly angels joined with him in his attempt to overthrow God. These angelic rebels were immediately expelled from the third heaven and were given an eternal sentence in hell, and in the end, are to be cast into the Lake of Fire. When tracking the future of Satan according to the Bible, it becomes clear that he either cannot repent as there is no repentance available to him or he and his rebels are only intent on destroying whomever they can and whatever they can in retaliation against God. Satan will one day come down with great wrath (Rev. 12) in an attempt to destroy the Jewish seed on the earth (Rev. 12). He will, however, be defeated at Armageddon and bound for a thousand years. Yet, after he is ejected from the abyss at the conclusion of the thousand years, he continues one more resistance against Christ and the saints (Rev. 20).

Spirits from ages past, including angels, have already set their eternal destiny as there is no repentance given to fallen angels. Fallen man, however, is different. Man is made in the image and likeness of God, and God desires that all humanity will be with Him in eternity as it is written, "God... is not willing that any perish but that all come to repentance" (2 Pet. 3:9). As long as your spirit remains in the body, there is an opportunity to repent. Once your spirit has permanently departed from the body, repentance opportunities no longer exist. This is why Satan, the fallen angels, and all evil spirits cannot, and because of their evil inclinations, will not ever repent.

Question: We see and meet many people from other religions who believe there is a God but use different names for Him. Many believe there is a heaven and even punishment for evil people in a place similar to hell. I cannot believe a "loving God" would allow anyone to go to hell as long as the person believes God exists. What do you think?

Answer: The belief that "all religions lead to heaven" is becoming common. If this were true, then why was it necessary for God to send His "only begotten son" to suffer, die, and be raised again? If just any religion leads to heaven, then the sacrifice of Christ was in vain and unnecessary.

The first point is that idol worship of false gods is idolatry. It is against the Ten Commandments and is forbidden throughout Scripture. Second, the Bible teaches that demons also believe in God and tremble (James 2:19). Believing there is a God is not the way to salvation and eternal life. Otherwise, demons could be "saved." Religion is useless energy if the religion is not founded on truth, specifically the truth of the Word of God. Salvation only comes through a "savior," and that Savior is Jesus Christ!

Question: I have heard you relate the belief that a spirit outside of the body can be transported from earth to heaven in a matter of seconds. Which, scientifically, is impossible. When expressing this theory to a non-believer, they mock you, saying it would be too cold in the outer universe to survive, there is no oxygen to breathe, and it is humanly impossible to move faster than the speed of light, which would take millions of years to reach heaven. What is your response to their argument?

Answer: First, no "unbeliever" has been outside of their body to disprove this (except for a possible near-death experience), and no unbeliever has traveled to the third heaven to measure the type of gases and molecules in the atmosphere that exists for spirits to operate in. Thus, the unbelief of a sinner is based upon the knowledge of science, which continues to learn, and whose researchers have yet to tap into God's third heaven realm.

Our evidence of the speed of travel can be observed when Enoch was translated to heaven (Gen. 5:24; Heb. 11:5) when Elijah was taken in a chariot from the plains of Nebo to heaven (2 Kings 2), and when Christ ascended from the Mount of Olives in Jerusalem and was later seen by Stephen, "standing, on the right hand (right side) of God" (Acts 1:9; Acts 7:55-56). John, in Revelation, wrote in symbolism about the two olive trees and two candlesticks (two prophets) who will be the two future witnesses on earth during the tribulation (Rev. 11:1-4). These two are believed by many scholars to be Enoch and Elijah, two men who have never died but will die, in Jerusalem, at the end of the first forty-two months of the tribulation. The point is, all three made it from earth to heaven, the moment of their departure, and it did not take millions of years!

As far as heat and the lack thereof, the human soul and spirit are of a different molecular structure than the human body and does not respond to the elements of hot and cold *in the same manner* an unprotected body would respond. Angels continually travel from earth to heaven without any injury as they are spirits. There is actually an angel who was given power over the sun and over fire (Rev. 16:8; 19:17). There are places on earth where the weather is 50 degrees below zero. Yet, angels need no special clothing when ministering in the sub-freezing zones around the globe.

The word 'spirit' in Hebrew is *ruwach* and is translated in the English Bible as wind, breath, and spirit. The breath of God came from God into Adam's new body of clay, and suddenly, Adam became a "living soul" (Gen. 2:7). He was not just a soul but a living soul. God's breath is the lifeforce of both the soul and the spirit, since the life of the soul is the breath of God, and God is a spirit (John 4:24). Oxygen is needed for the blood as blood is the "life of the flesh" (Lev. 17:11).

The point is this: movement from earth to heaven has already been tested and is occurring every day with angelic messengers. We do not understand all of the mysteries linked with this process, but certainly accept, as a fact, the Biblical narratives that demonstrate how this is possible.

CONCLUSION

One word that can sum up this book is the word CHOICE. Man is often called "a free, moral agent," meaning the ability to receive eternal life or remain under the eternal penalty of death is a choice each person must make after hearing the Gospel of redemption from sin. Joshua said it well when he said:

> "And if it seem evil unto you to serve the Lord, choose you this day whom ye will serve; whether the gods which your fathers served that were on the other side of the flood or the gods of the Amorites, in whose land ye dwell: but as for me and my house, we will serve the Lord.
>
> - JOSHUA 24:15

The choice to serve the Lord begins by acknowledging that you are under the law of sin and death, and the only way to be released is to ask God to forgive your sins through Christ's sacrifice and enter into a redemptive covenant with Christ. This covenant means that you will follow the Lord, His Word, and His instruction all the days of your life. You will "choose to serve the Lord."

God has never "sent anyone to hell," as anyone remaining under the sin and death penalty without removing it, sets their own destination. Receiving Christ and following Him is your guarantee of resting in the third heaven after your death.

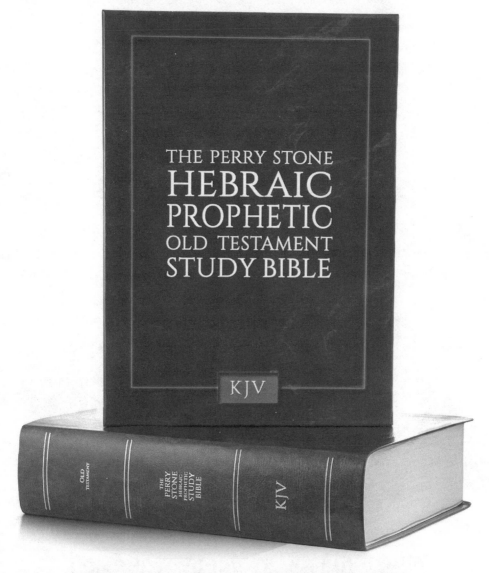

THE PERRY STONE HEBRAIC PROPHETIC NEW TESTAMENT STUDY BIBLE

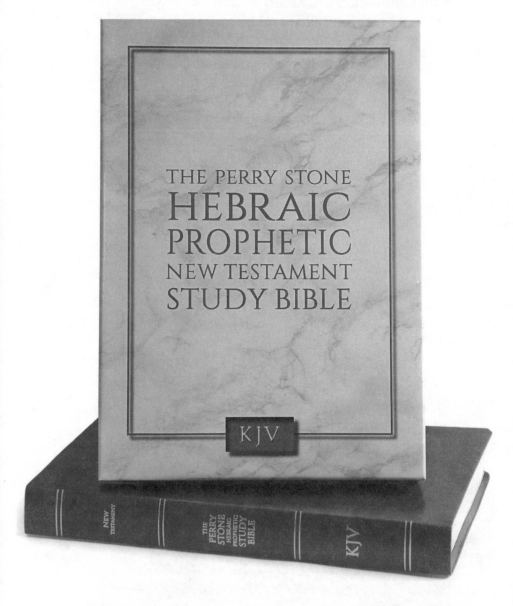

ORDER ONLINE AT PERRYSTONE.ORG
OR CALL (423) 478.3456